SwitchBoard™

A Treasure Chest of Reproducible Templates

Concept and Development
Miguel Kagan

Designer: Heather Malk
Illustrator: Erin Kant
Publications Manager: Becky Herrington

Kagan

© 2012 by **Kagan Publishing**

This book is published by **Kagan Publishing**. All rights are reserved by **Kagan Publishing**. No part of this publication may be reproduced or transmitted in any form by any means, electronic or mechanical, including photocopy, recording, or any information storage and retrieval system, without prior written permission from **Kagan Publishing**. The blackline masters included in this book are intended for duplication only by classroom teachers who purchase the book, for use limited to their own classrooms. To obtain additional copies of this book, or information regarding professional development, contact:

Kagan Publishing
981 Calle Amanecer
San Clemente, CA 92673
1 (800) 933-2667
www.KaganOnline.com

ISBN: 978-1-933445-24-3

Introduction

This book is a treasure chest of reproducible templates. Between the covers, you'll find more than 300 templates across the curriculum as well as a variety of learning templates and games. These ready-to-use templates are great time savers for you and your students. Simply copy a template for each student or team, and they are ready to use. You can use the templates as individual worksheets or as slip-in templates for a dry-erase marker pouch (see SwitchBoard on the next page). Together, this large collection of templates provides a rich array of ideas and activities to help you teach a wide range of learning concepts.

In This Treasure Chest You Will Find…

The templates are divided into seven categories by "best fit." However, as you look through these templates, you will see many of them can be used with multiple subjects. Most of the templates are generic, providing you with the extra flexibility to use them in many different ways.

Graphic Organizers
Use graphic organizers to help students visually represent their knowledge and understanding. They'll learn thinking skills as they map out the curriculum. You'll find straightforward templates for comparing and contrasting, sequencing, identifying cause and effect, and many more core thinking skills.

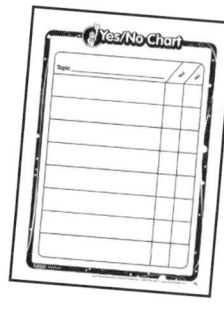

Mathematics
Boost students' mathematical skills with these helpful templates. Students can mark the length of an object on their rulers, practice fact families, circle the coins that match a given value, and shade the fractions on the fraction bars or circles. You'll find an abundance of math templates to use over and over.

Language Arts
Develop literacy skills with these ready-to-use templates. Some of the reproducibles you'll find include a Character Chart to map out story characters, a template for students to write acrostic poems, and a Vocabulary Terms sheet for students to write, draw, and define vocabulary terms.

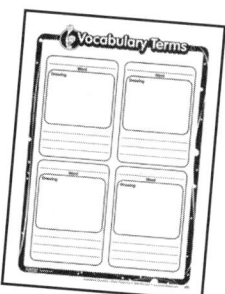

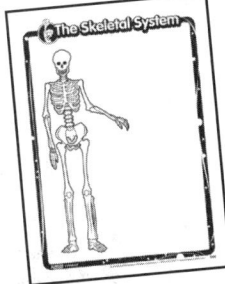

Science
Introduce your students to key concepts in science. Use the diagram of The Skeletal System to have students identify bones. Use the Water Cycle graphic to label and discuss the water cycle. Use the Animal Web sheet to explore animals in detail.

Introduction continued

Social Studies
Promote an understanding of humans and the world we live in with these Social Studies templates. You'll find maps of the world, states, and countries to help students develop geography skills. Also included are timelines that help students map out the sequence of historical events. Plus, you'll discover a Current Event sheet students can use to research and report on current events.

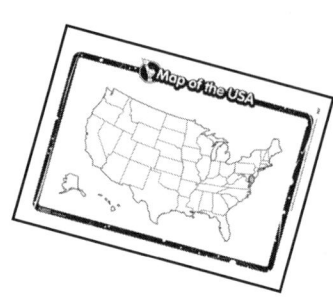

Response Cards
Promote active engagement by every student. Instead of asking for one student to answer, have every student answer using their own response cards. Response Cards can also be used by student teams to show their team's response to the question. You'll find response cards covering the most frequent classroom questions, including Multiple Choice, Fact or Opinion, True/False, and Agree/Disagree.

Games
Teach using some classic games for your students to play. If you're looking for a fun activity or a way to build logic skills, check out some of these favorites. Students can play Hangman, Tic-Tac-Toe, Four in a Row, and more!

SwitchBoard
The Switchable Write-N-Wipe Board

The templates in this book were designed as slip-in sheets for SwitchBoard. SwitchBoard is a plastic write-n-wipe pouch designed to switch out the inserts easily. When it's time to compare and contrast, students unzip their SwitchBoards and place the Venn Diagram insert as the top sheet inside the transparent pouch. They now have a graphic organizer they can fill in using a dry-erase marker. When done with the activity, they simply wipe their SwitchBoard pouches clean. With SwitchBoard, you can turn any sheet in this book into a dry-erase sheet! SwitchBoard's zipper pouch allows students to store those frequently used worksheets and templates so they are always within reach.

Table of Contents

- Introduction 3

Graphic Organizers and Templates

- 2x2 Matrix 9
- 5W Chart 11
- 5W Flower 13
- Bookmark 15
- Cartoon Strip—4 Cell 17
- Cause/Effect 19
- Cause/Effect Diagram 23
- Cause/Effect Fishbone 25
- CD Design 27
- Certificate 29
- Checklist 31
- Compare/Contrast Chart 33
- Comparison Chart 35
- Concept Map 37
- Concept Wheel 39
- Cycle Graph 41
- Draw and Tell Journal 43
- Know, Wonder, Learned (KWL) 45
- List of 10 47
- Pyramid 49
- Same-Different Map 51
- Sequence Chain 53
- Sequence (Filmstrip) 55
- Six Questions 57
- Sorting Boxes 59
- Sorting Buckets 61
- Stepladder 63
- To Do List 65
- Triple Venn Diagram 67
- Venn Diagram 69
- Word and Definition 71
- Yes/No Chart 73

Mathematics

- Addition Problems 77
- Bar Chart 79
- Bar Graph Template 83
- Base 10 85
- Base 10 Grid Paper 87
- Base 10 Mat 89
- Clock 91
- Coins 95
- Coordinate Grid 10x10 99
- Division Problems 101
- Dots 103
- Fact Family—Addition/Subtraction 105
- Fact Family—Multiplication/Division . . . 107
- Fractions 109
- Function Tables 117
- Graph Paper 119
- Greater Than, Less Than, Equal To 121
- Hundred Number Chart 123
- Isometric Dot Pattern 125
- Multiplication Array 127
- Multiplication Mat 1–9 129
- Multiplication Mat 1–12 131
- Multiplication Problems 133
- Place Value Mat 135
- Place Value Mat—Decimals 139
- Rulers—Centimeters 141
- Rulers—Inches 145
- Shapes 149
- Subtraction Problems 151
- Symmetry 153
- Time 155
- Triangle Fact Family 157

Language Arts

- Acrostic Poem 161
- Biography Map 163
- Biography Star Chart 165
- Character Chart 167
- Chart 171
- Cursive 173
- Cursive—Lowercase . . 175
- Cursive—Uppercase . . 177

Table of Contents *continued*

- Descriptive Writing Star 179
- Journal Response 181
- Lined Paper 183
- Main Idea 187
- Outline 189
- Paragraph 193
- Parts of Speech 195
- Printing 197
- Printing—Lowercase 199
- Printing—Uppercase 201
- Story Hamburger 203
- Story Map 205
- Story Plot Map 207
- Vocabulary Term 209
- Vocabulary Terms 211
- Vocabulary Word 213

Science

- Animal Cell 217
- Animal Traits 219
- Animal Web 221
- Cycle Graph 223
- Four Seasons 225
- Solar System 227
- The Skeletal System 229
- Volcano 231
- Water Cycle 233

Social Studies

- Conflict Map 237
- Country Facts 239
- Current Event 241
- Democrats vs. Republicans 243
- Event Timeline 245
- Famous Explorer 247
- Gratefulness Journal 249
- Holiday 251
- Map of Africa 253
- Map of Antarctica 255
- Map of Asia 257
- Map of Australia 259
- Map of Europe 261
- Map of North America 263
- Map of South America 265
- Map of the USA 267
- State Facts 269
- Three Branches of Government 271
- Timeline 273
- U.S. President 277
- War 279
- World Leader 281
- World Map 283
- World Religion 285

Response Cards

- Agree-Disagree Scale 289
- Agree/Disagree 291
- Fact or Opinion 293
- Multiple Choice 295
- True/False 297
- Yes/No 299

Games

- Battleship 303
- Bulls and Cows—3-Digit 305
- Bulls and Cows—4-Digit 307
- Capture Boxes 309
- Five in a Row 313
- Four in a Row 315
- Hangman 317
- Making Words 319
- Pipe Layer 321
- Sudoku 4x4 323
- Sudoku 6x6 325
- Sudoku 9x9 327
- Tic-Tac-Toe 329

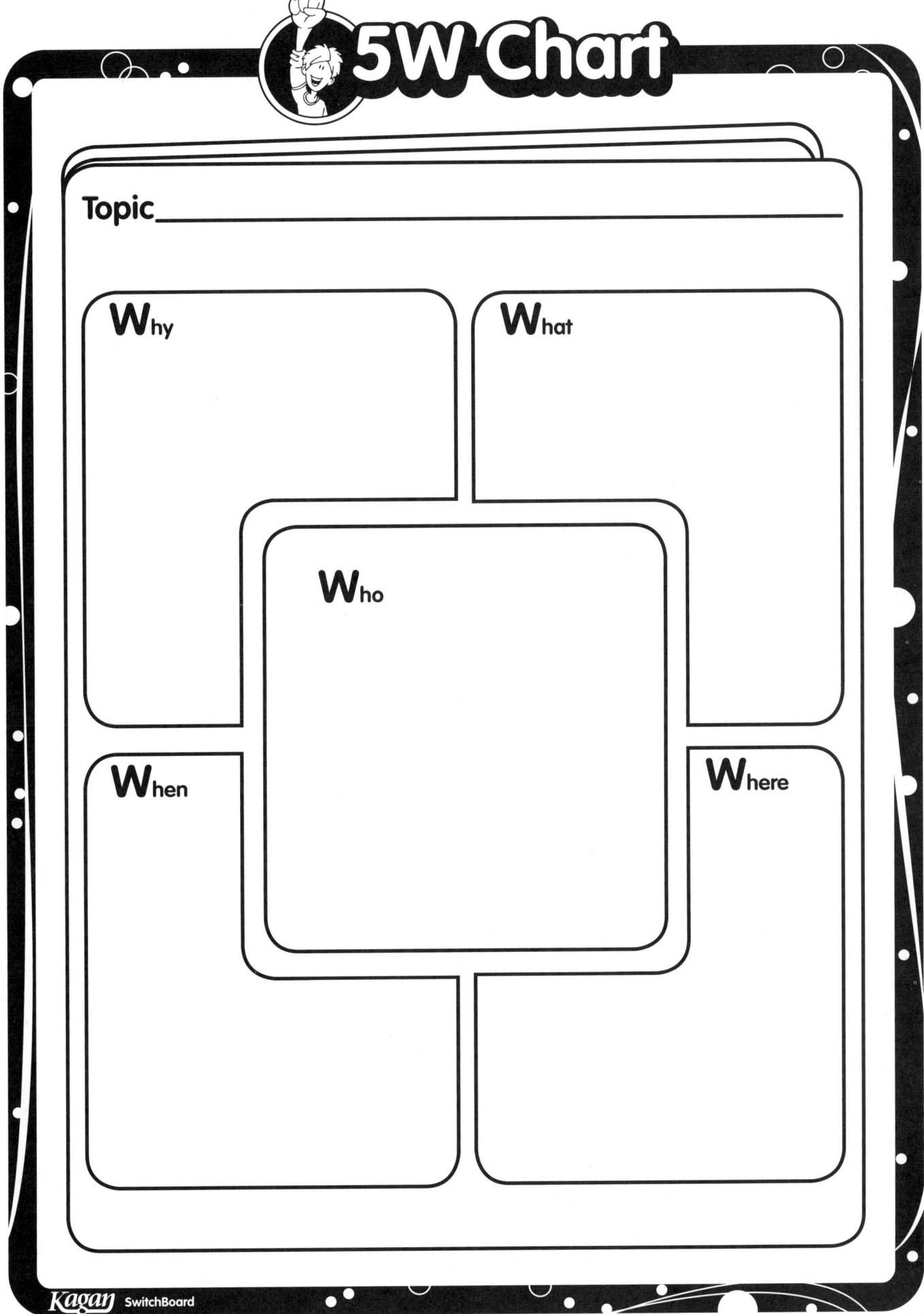

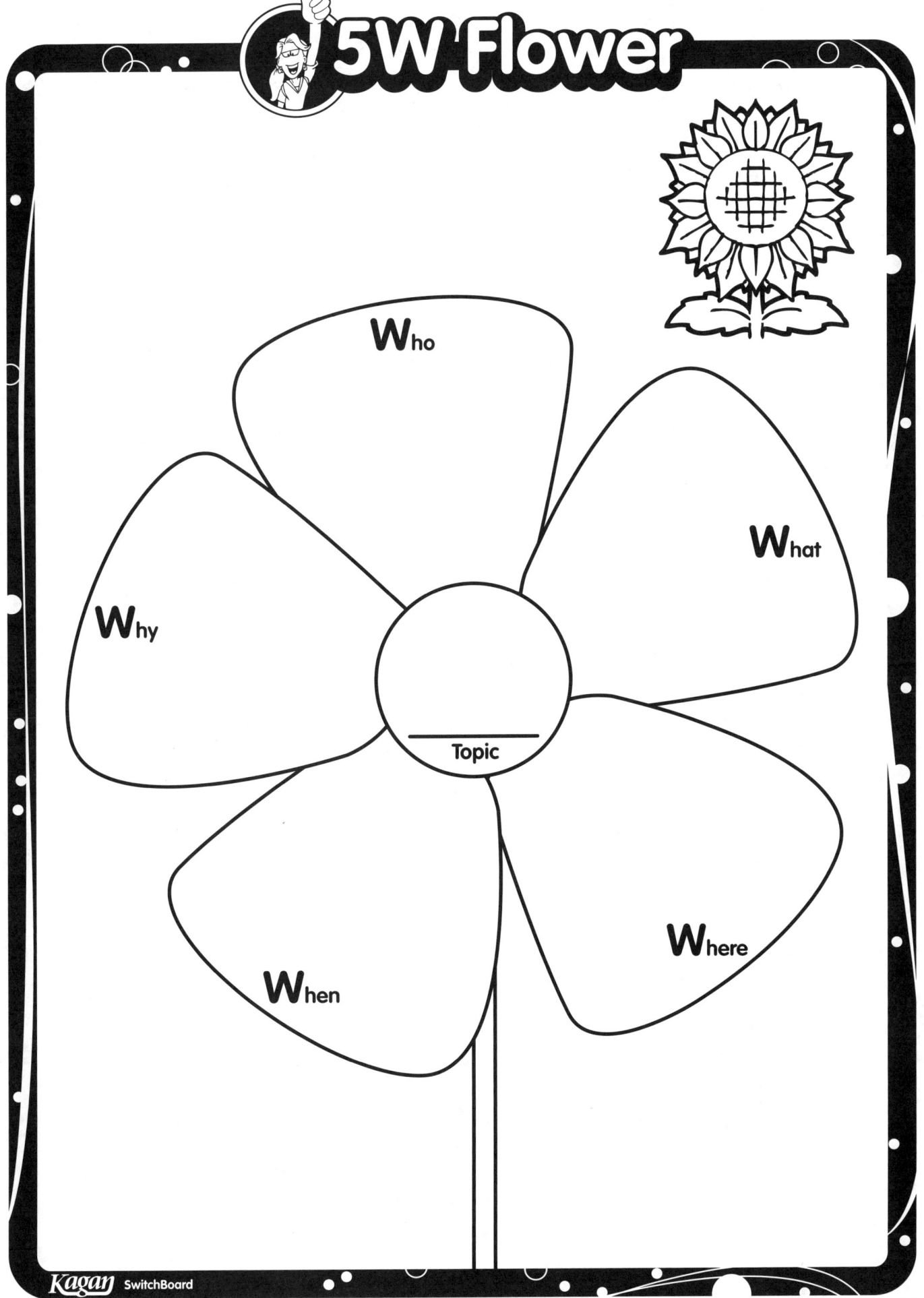

Topic _____

Front   Back

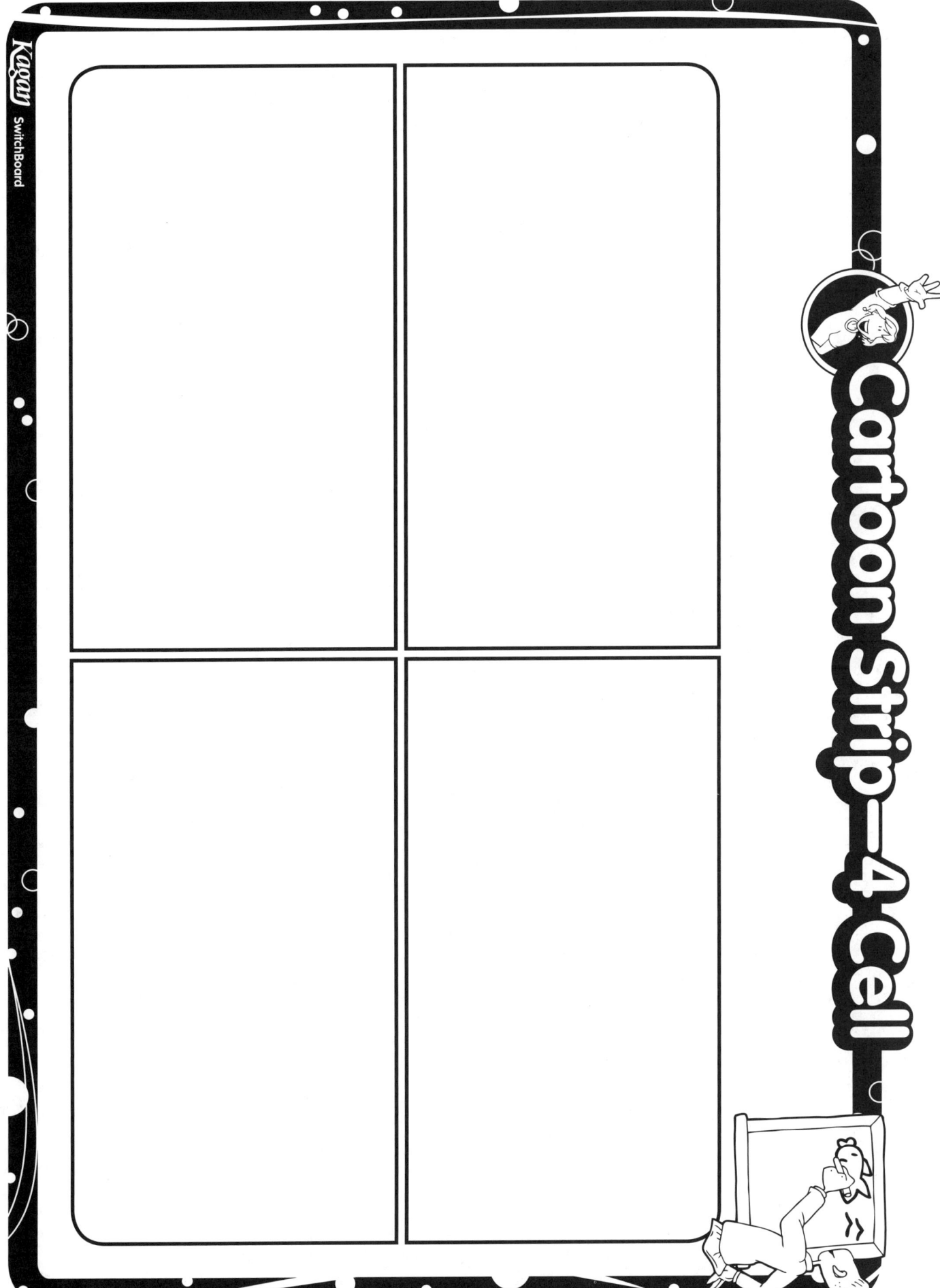

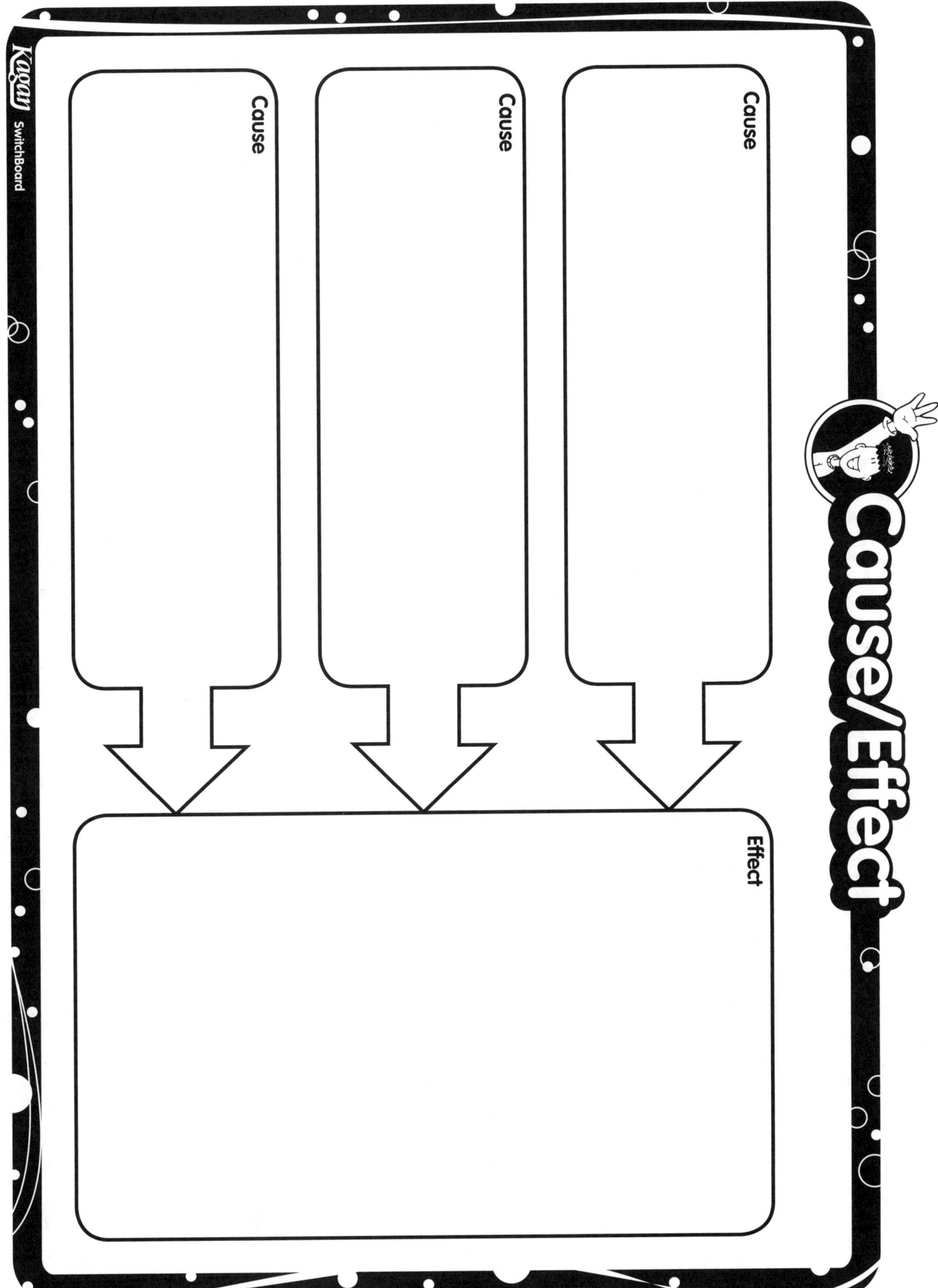

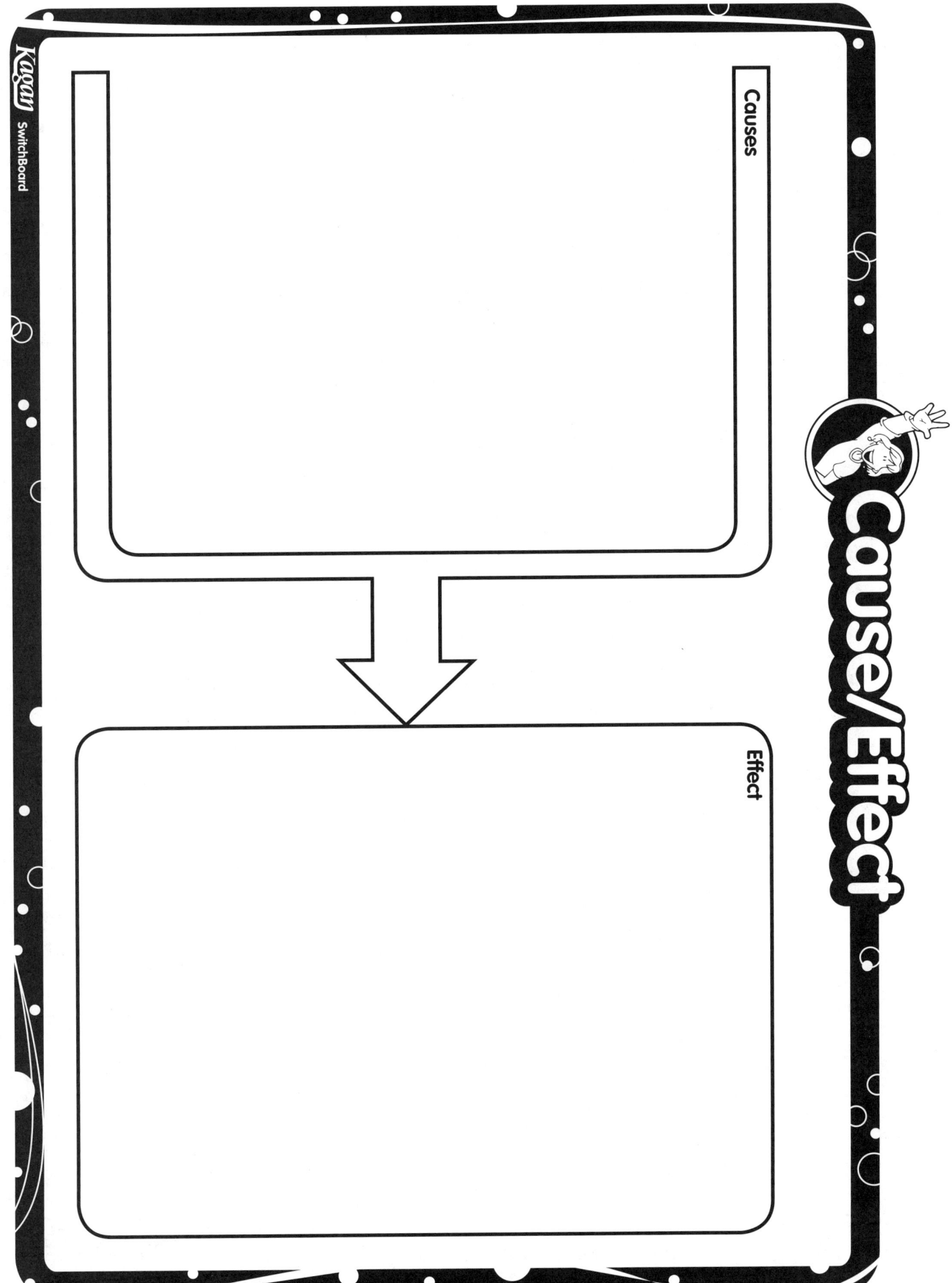

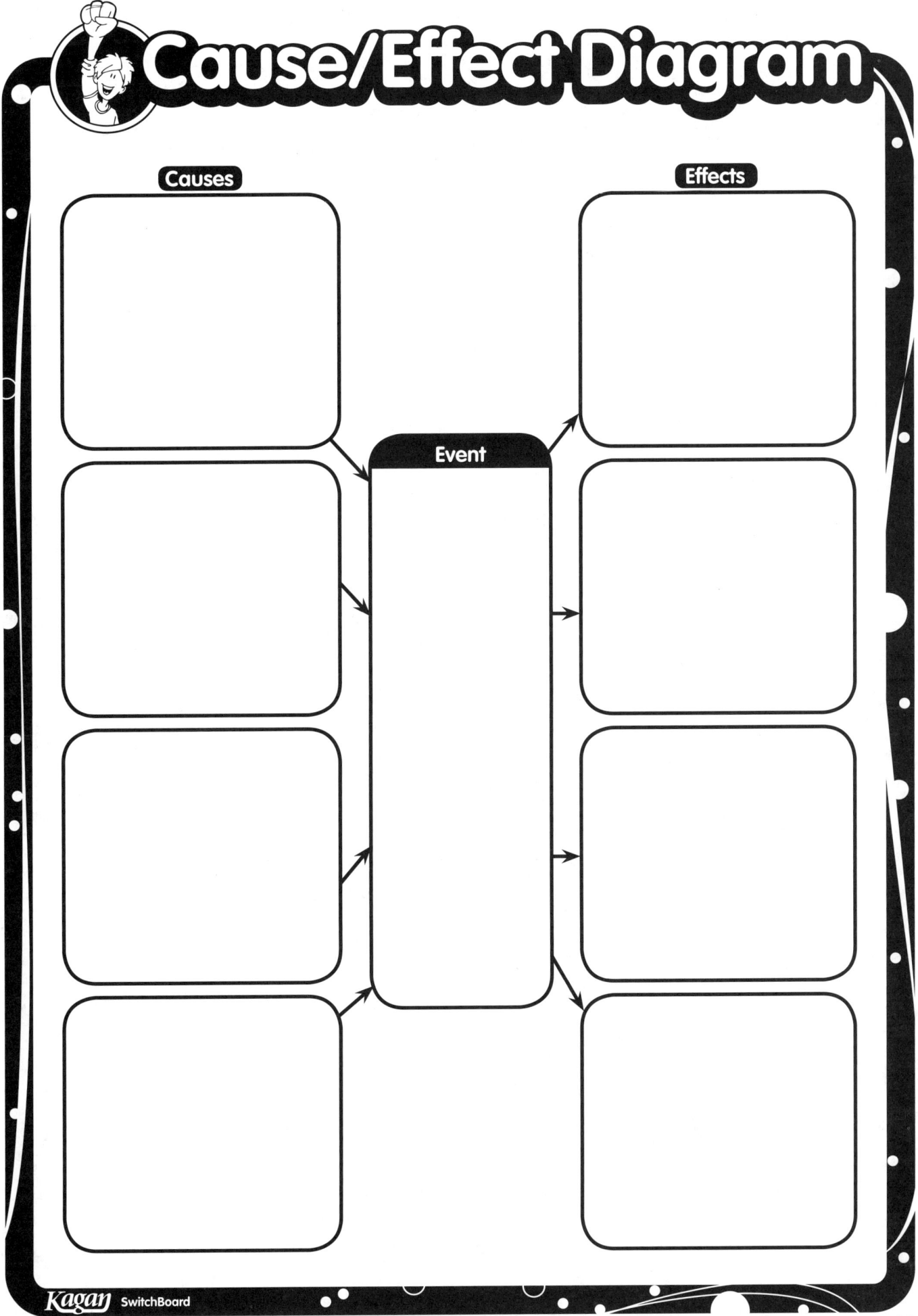

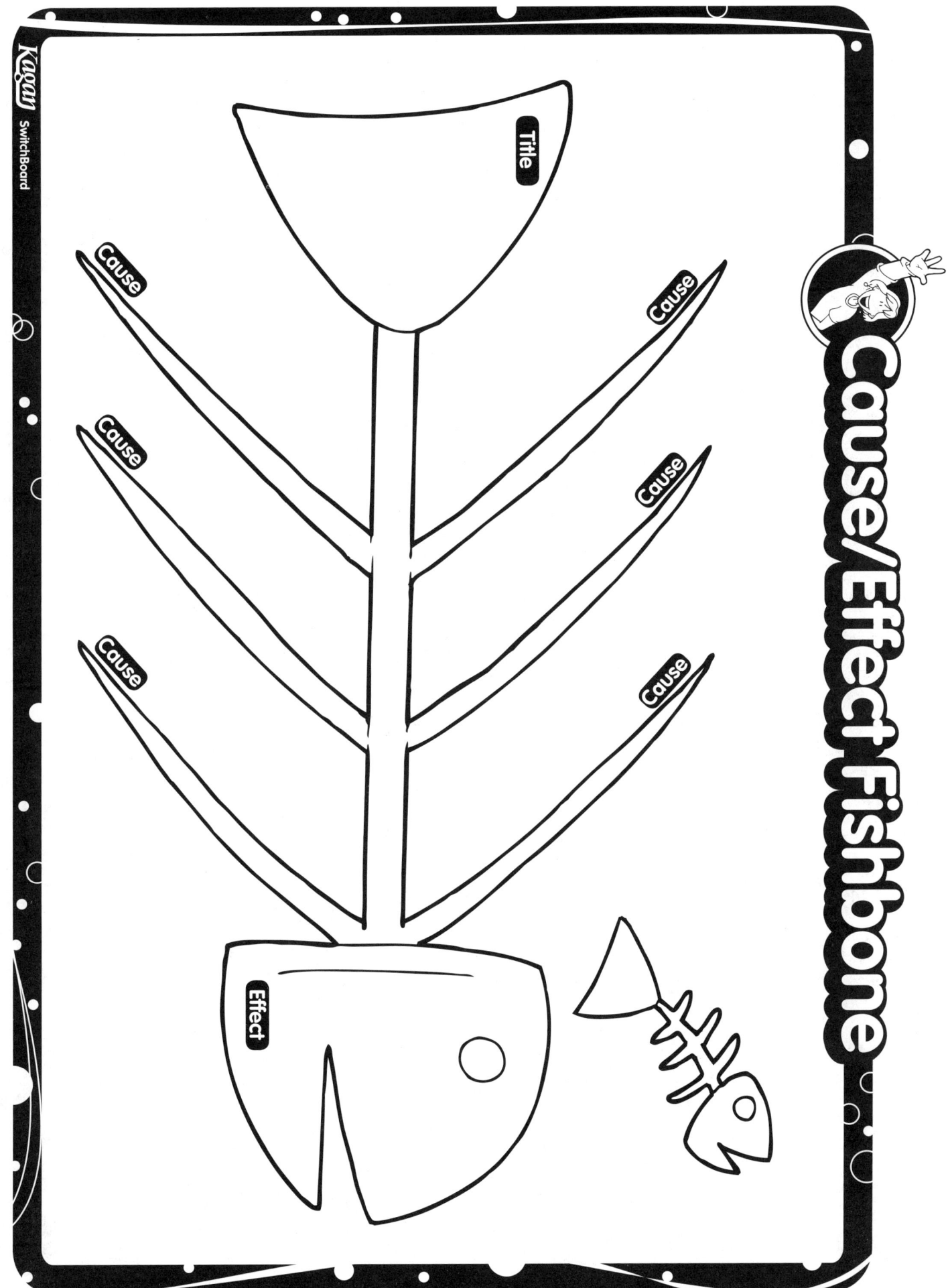

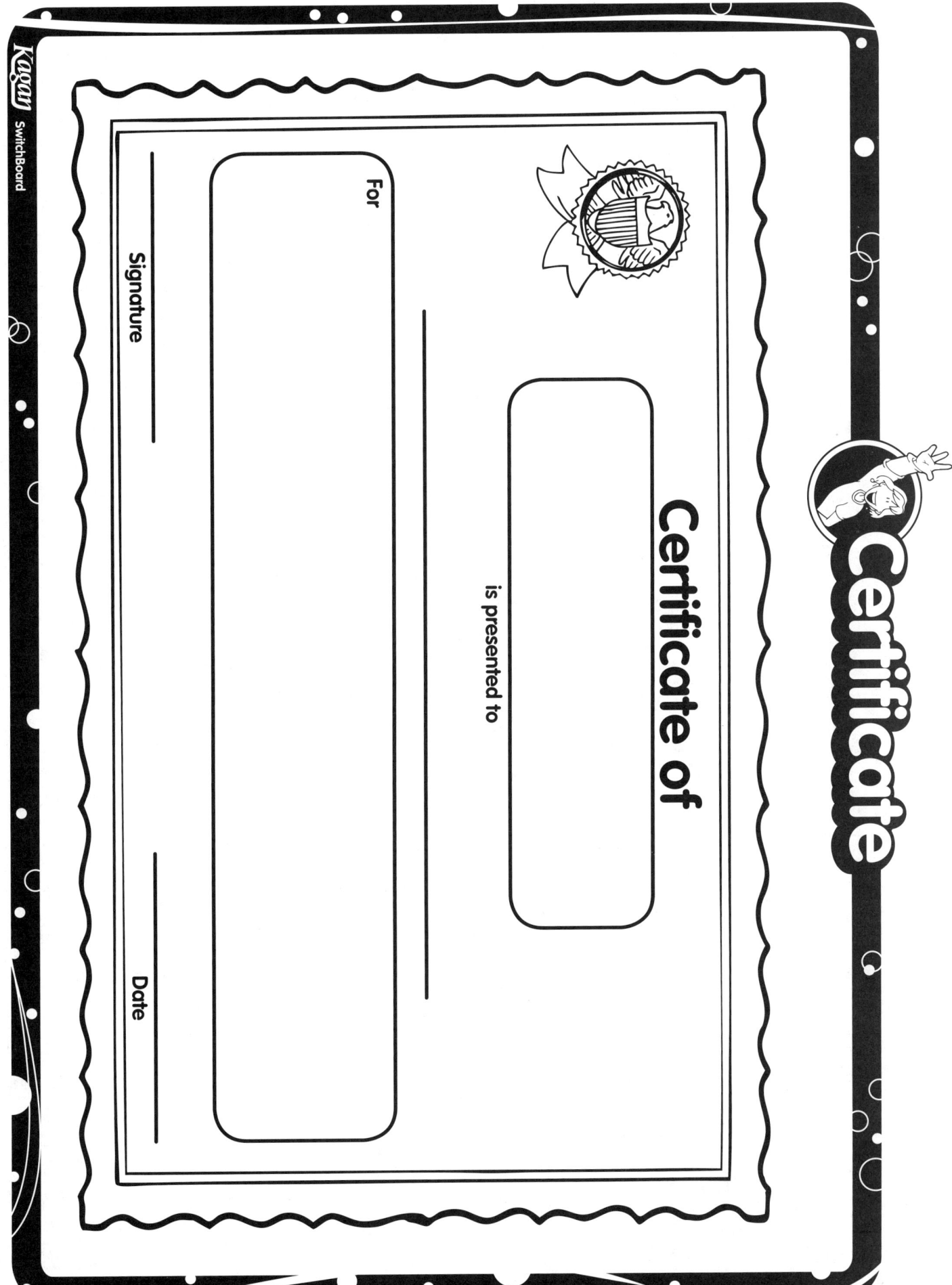

Topic_____

- ☐ _____
- ☐ _____
- ☐ _____
- ☐ _____
- ☐ _____

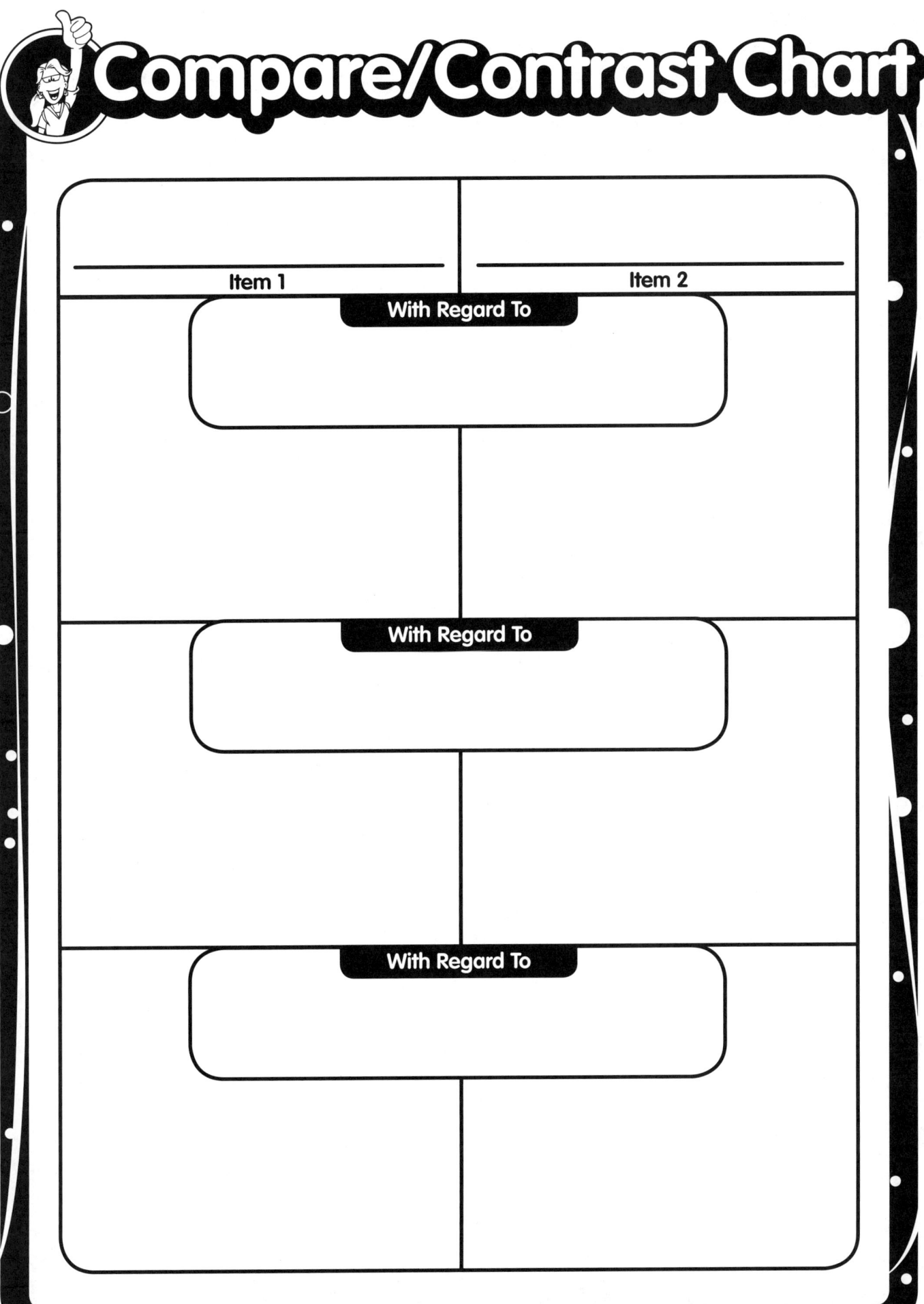

Comparison Chart

_____ vs _____
     Item 1   Item 2

Same	Different

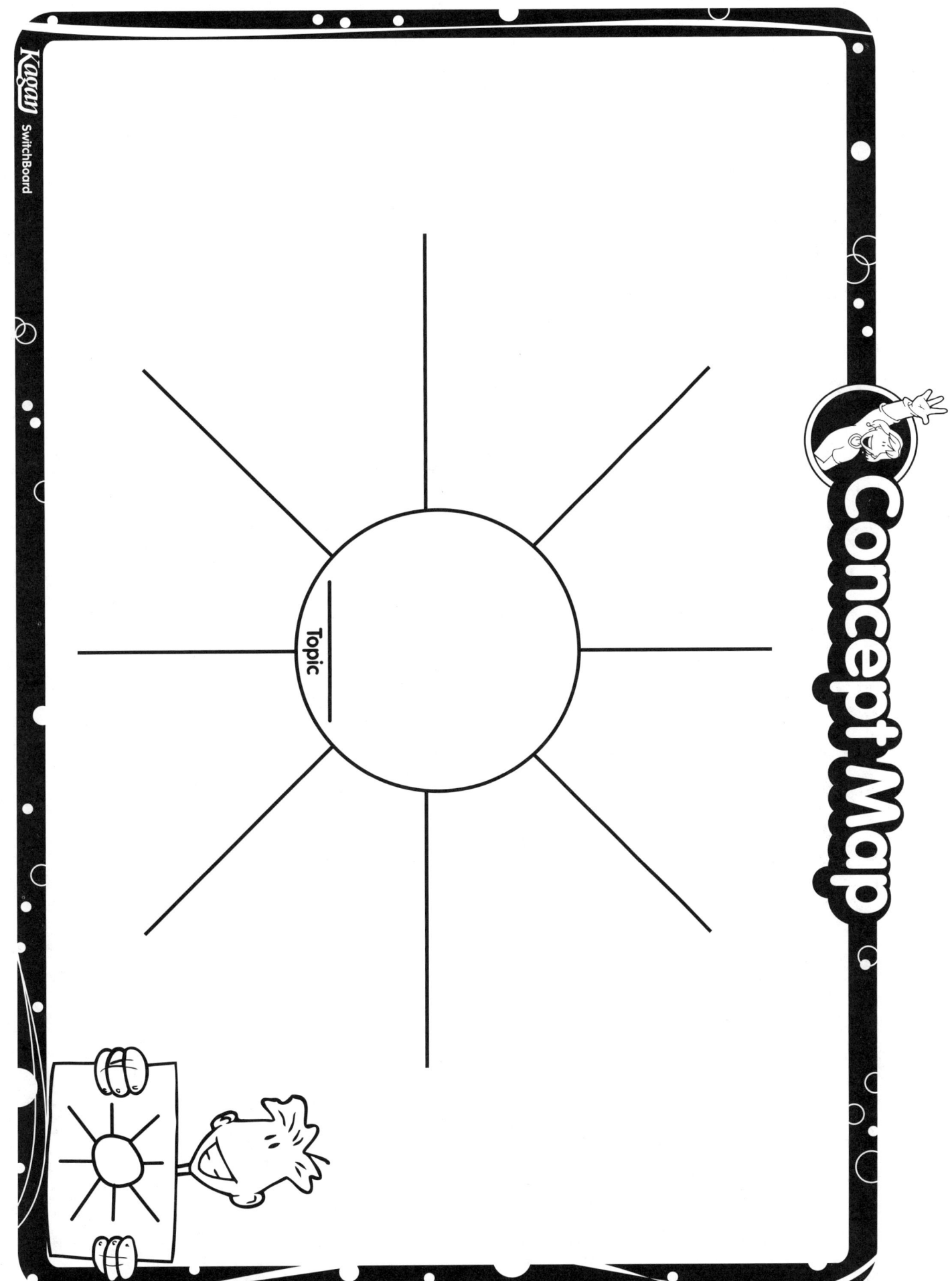

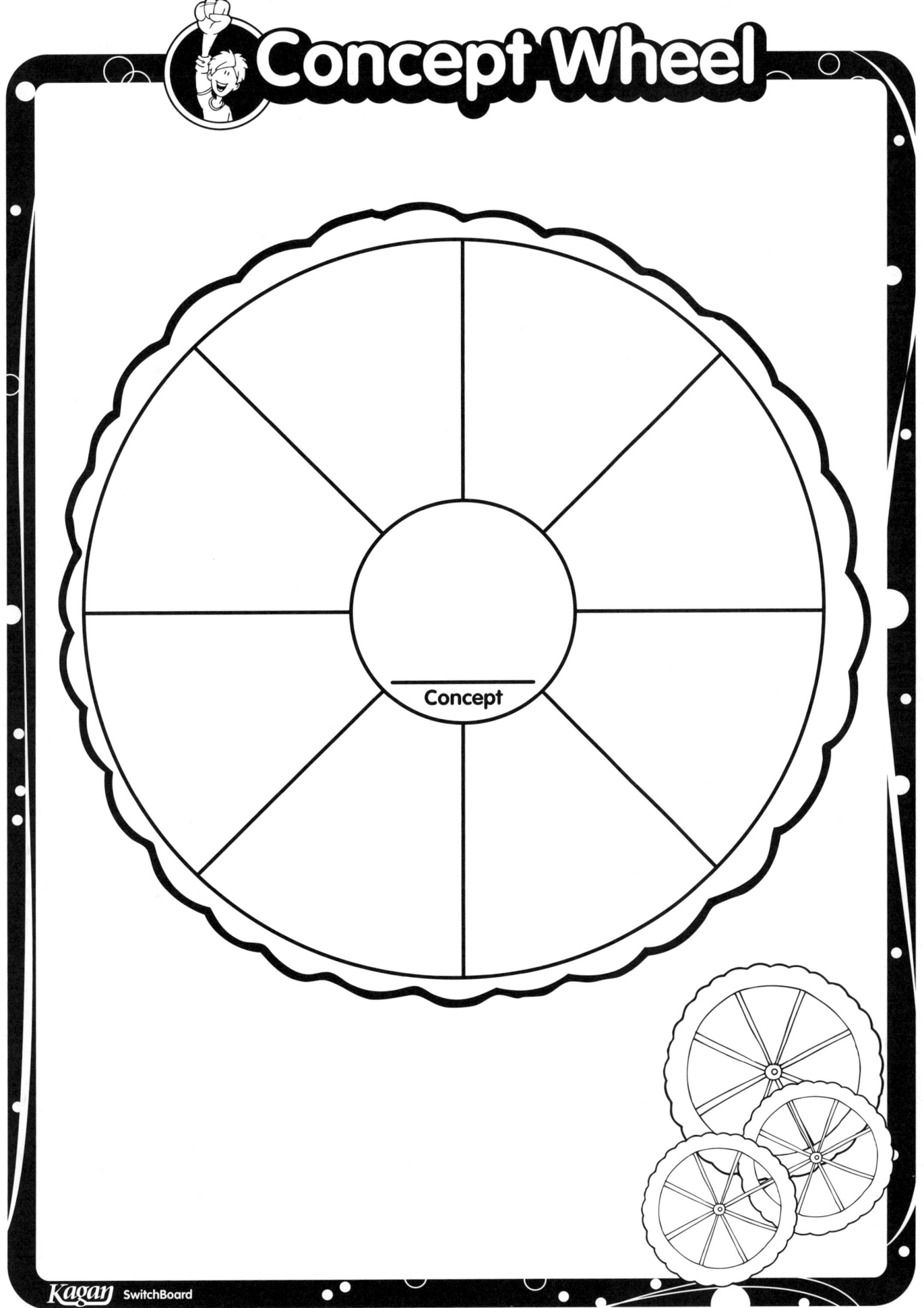

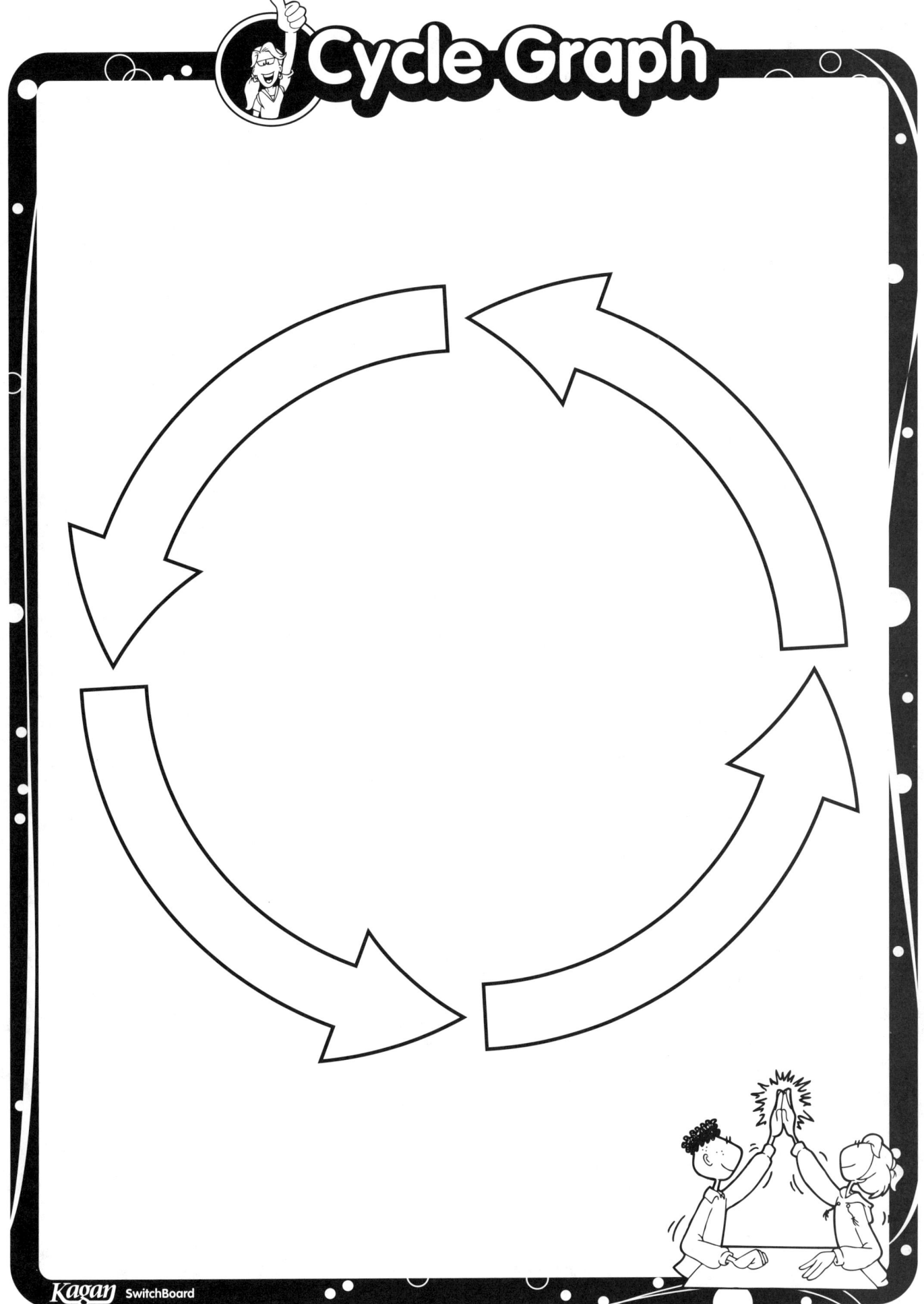

Draw and Tell Journal

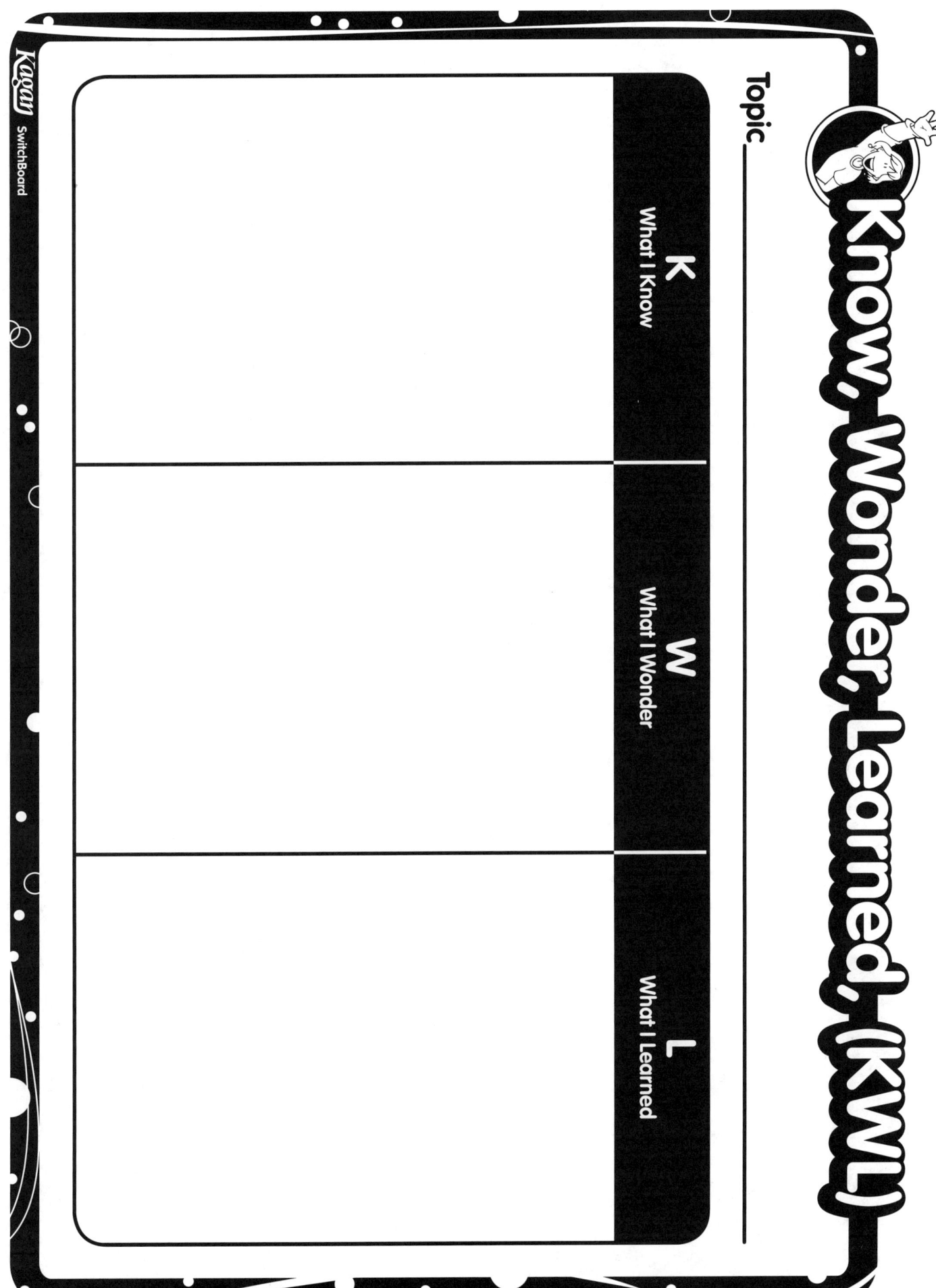

List of 10

Topic _____

10

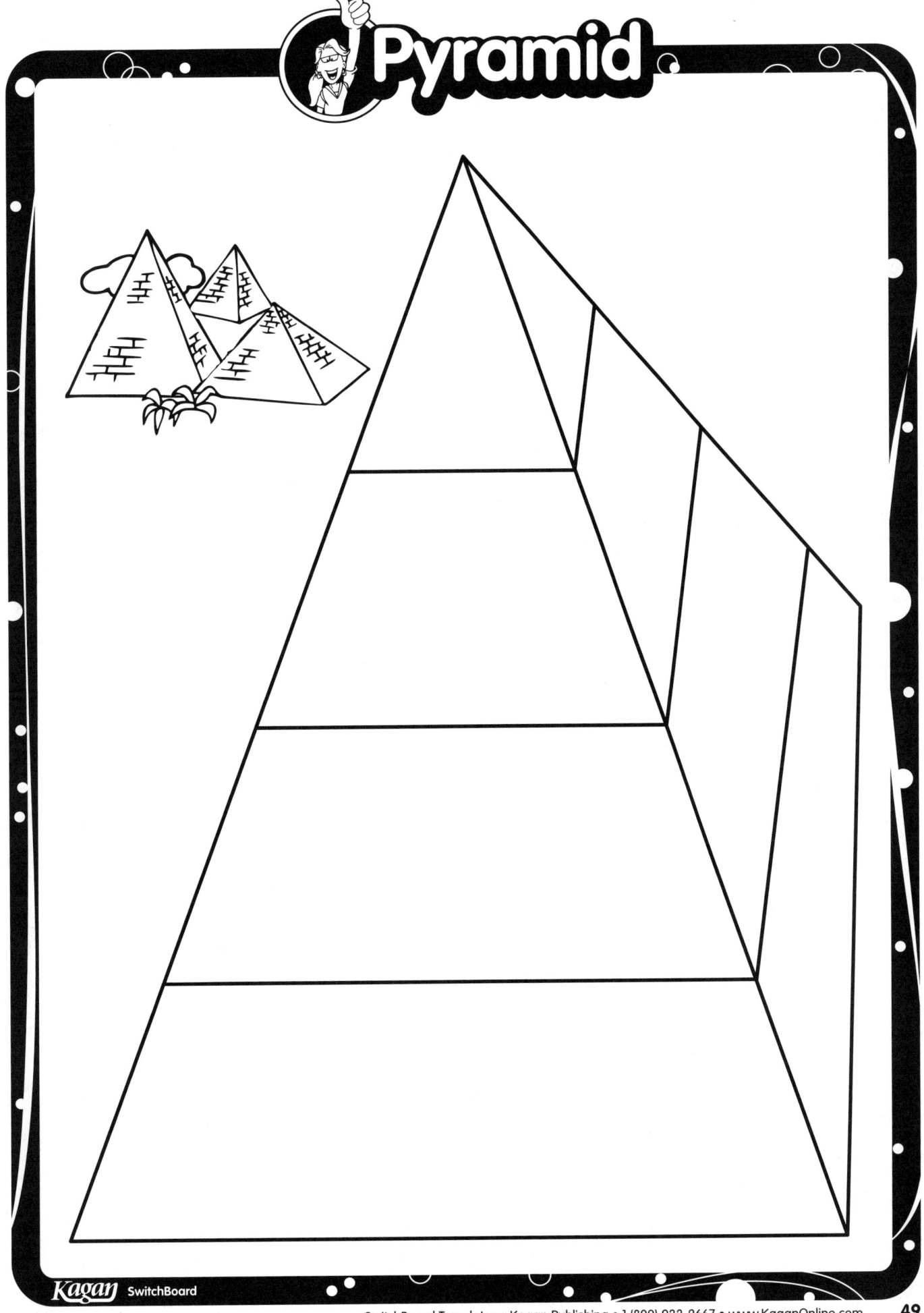

Same-Different Map

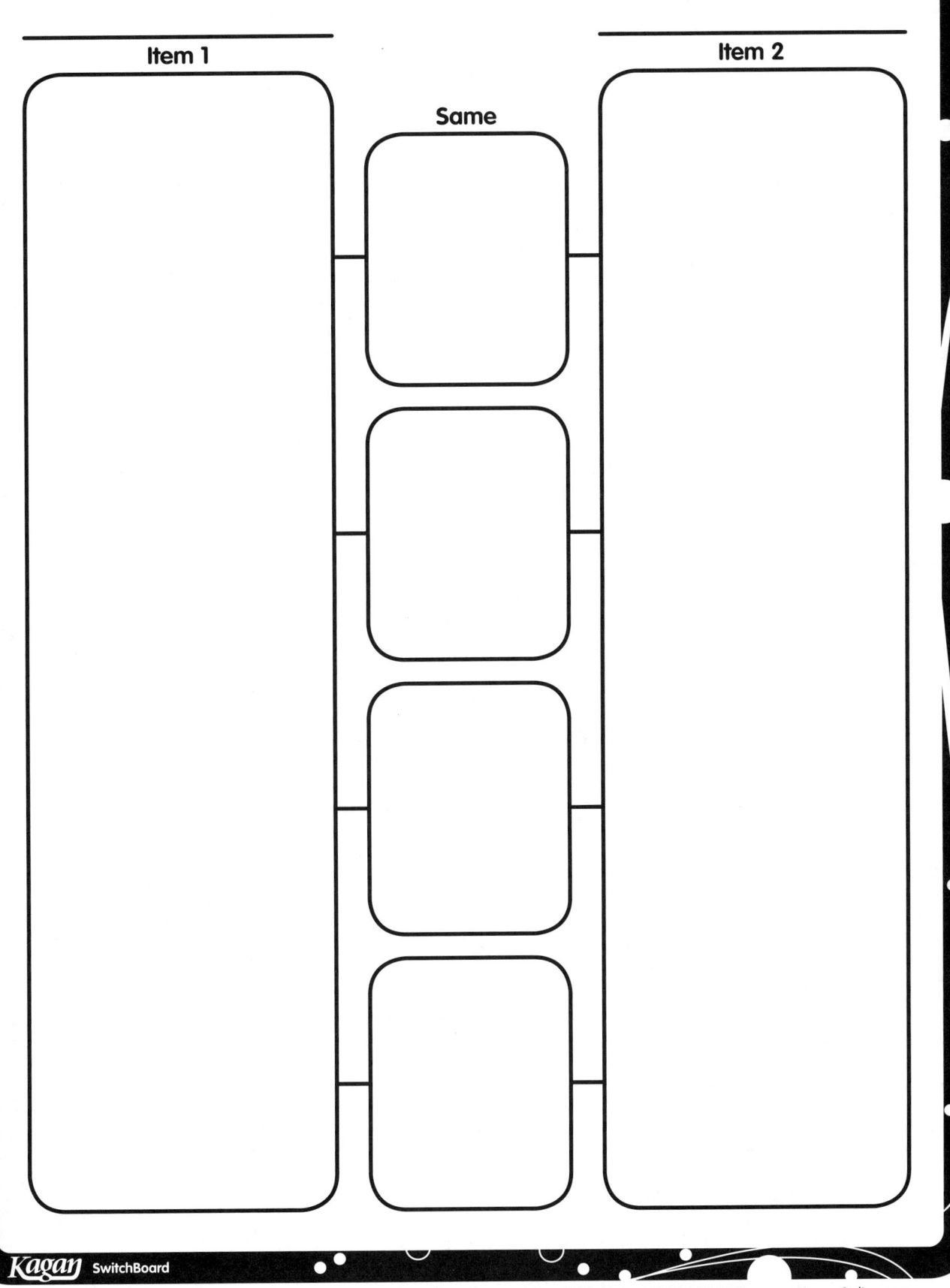

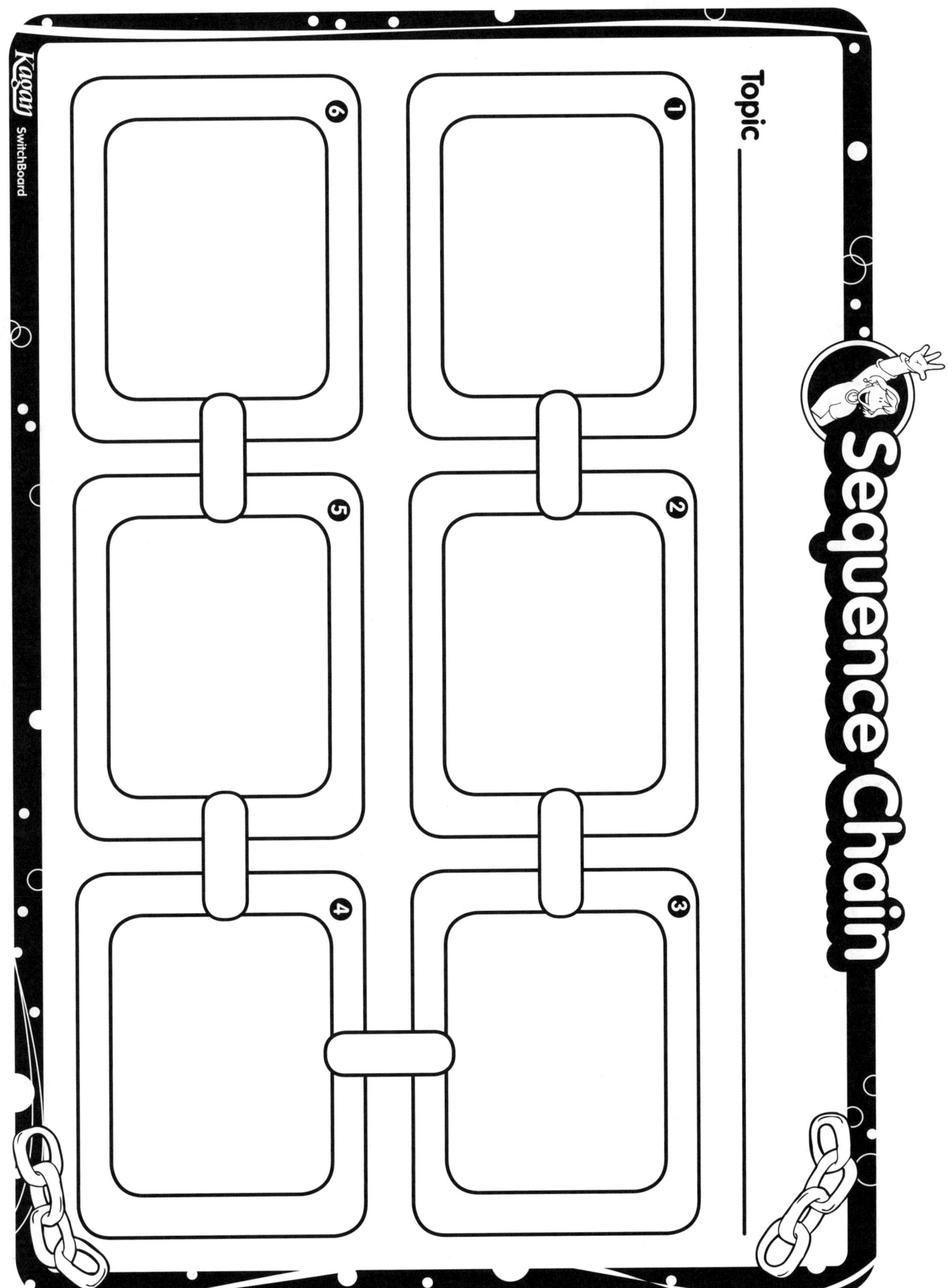

Topic _____

Who?	When?
What?	Why?
Where?	How?

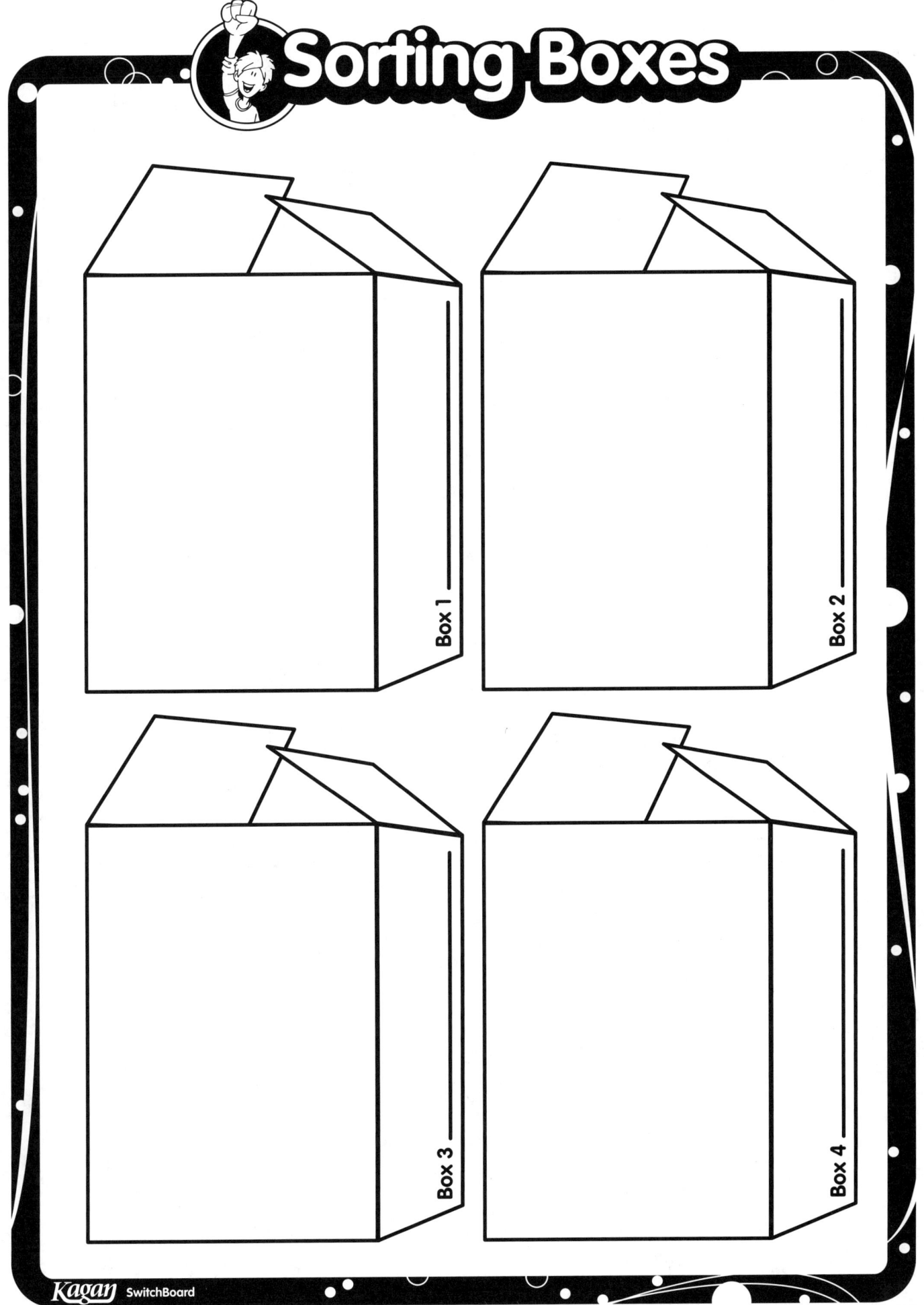

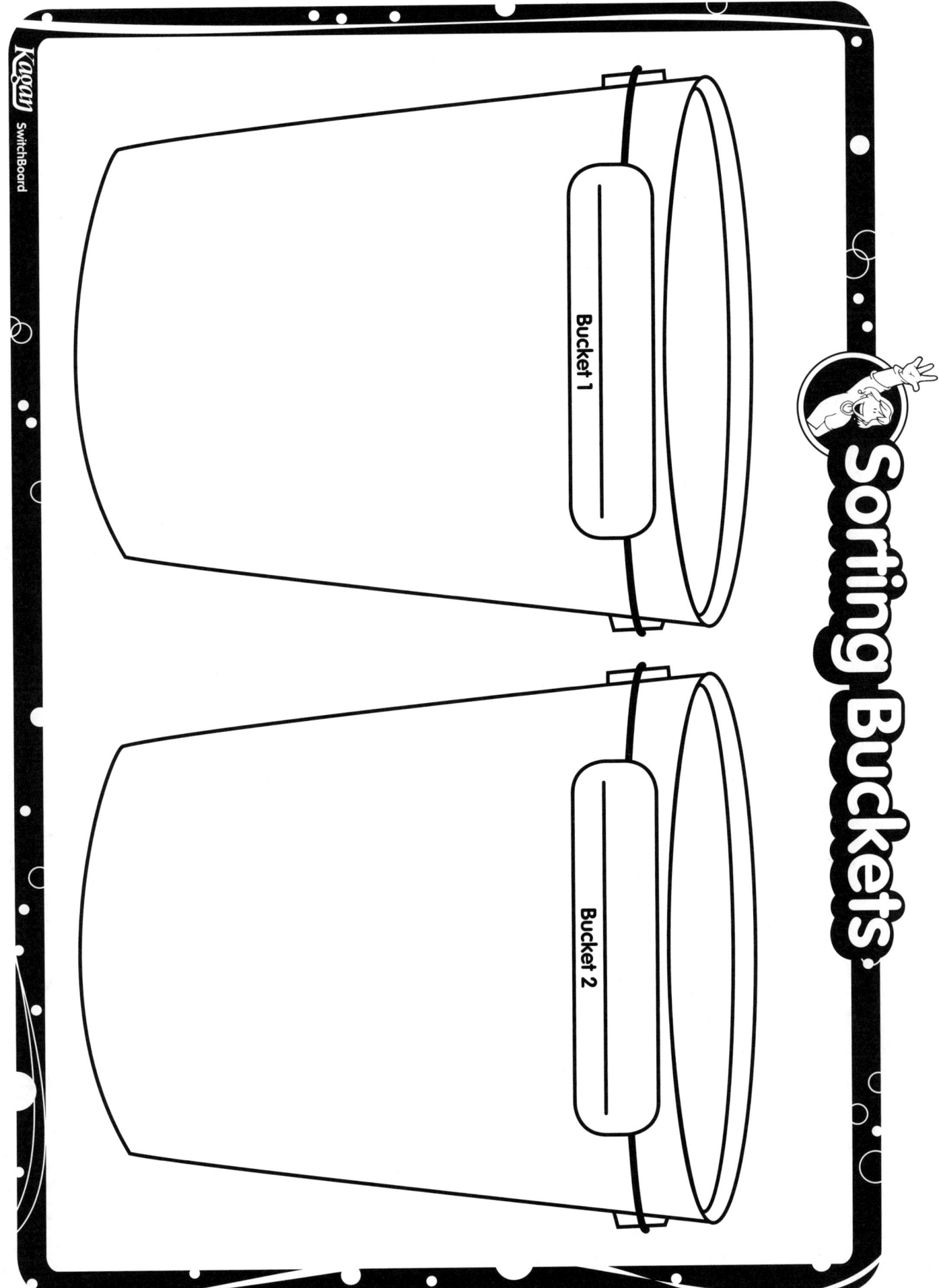

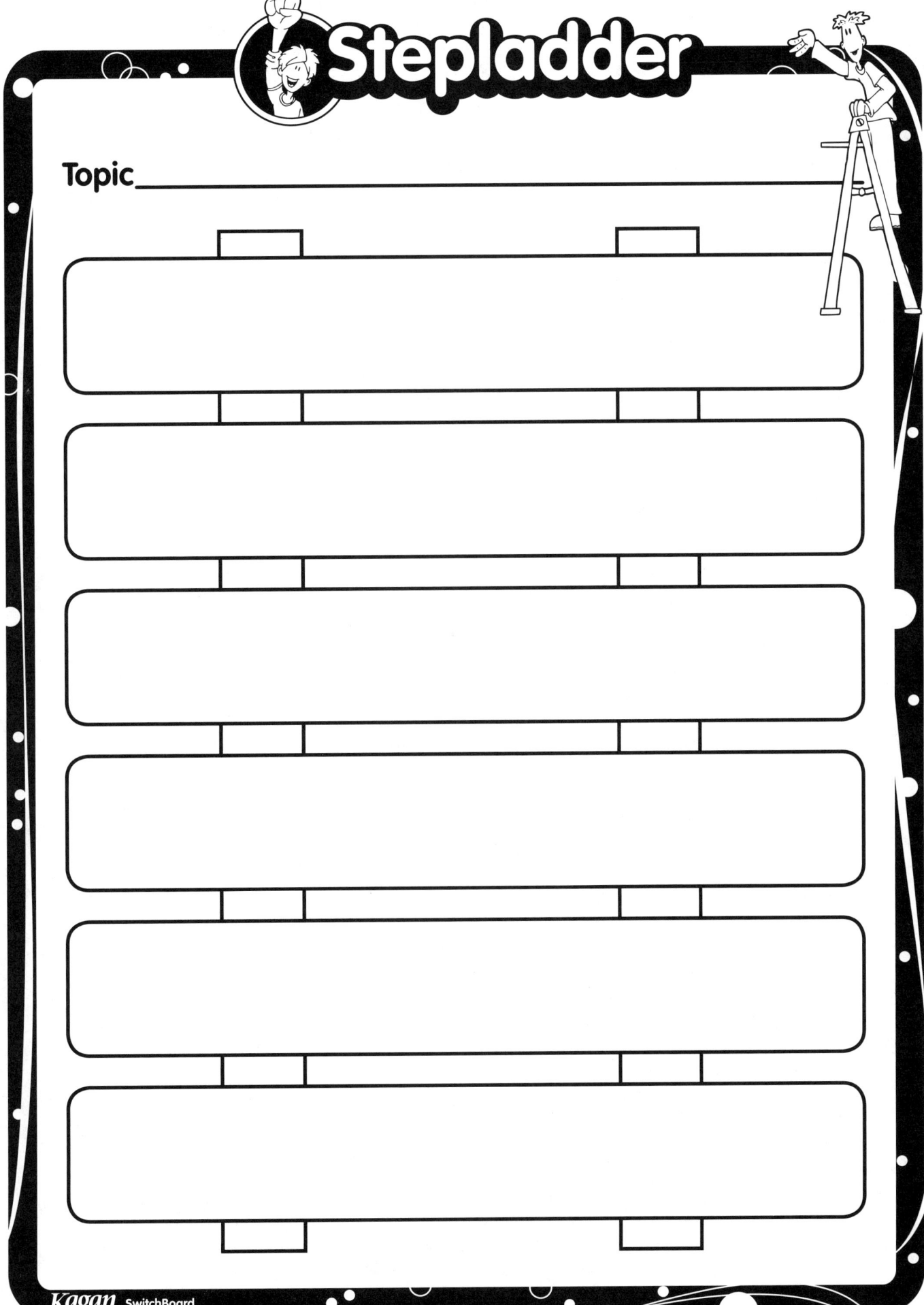

Triple Venn Diagram

Topic_____

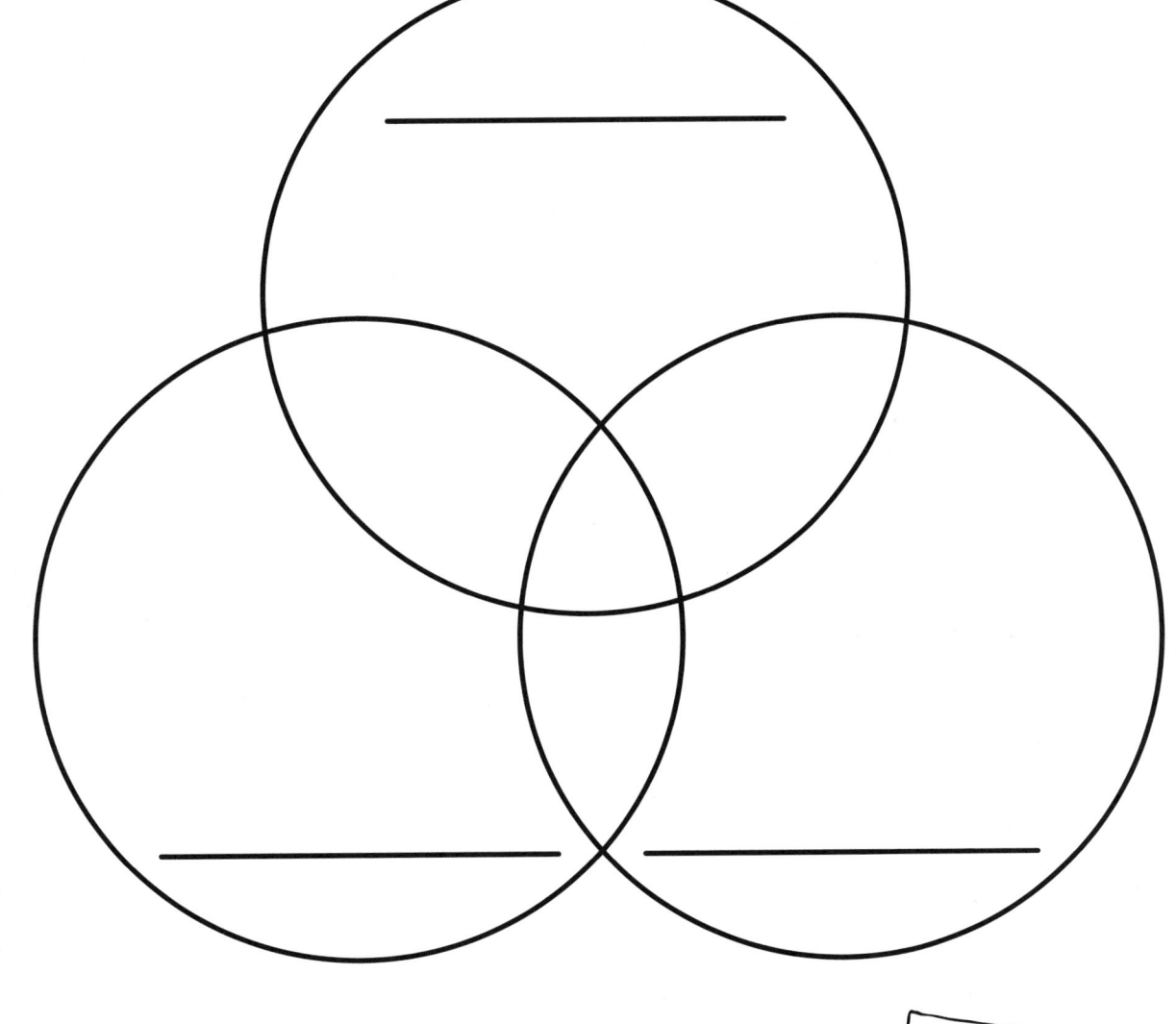

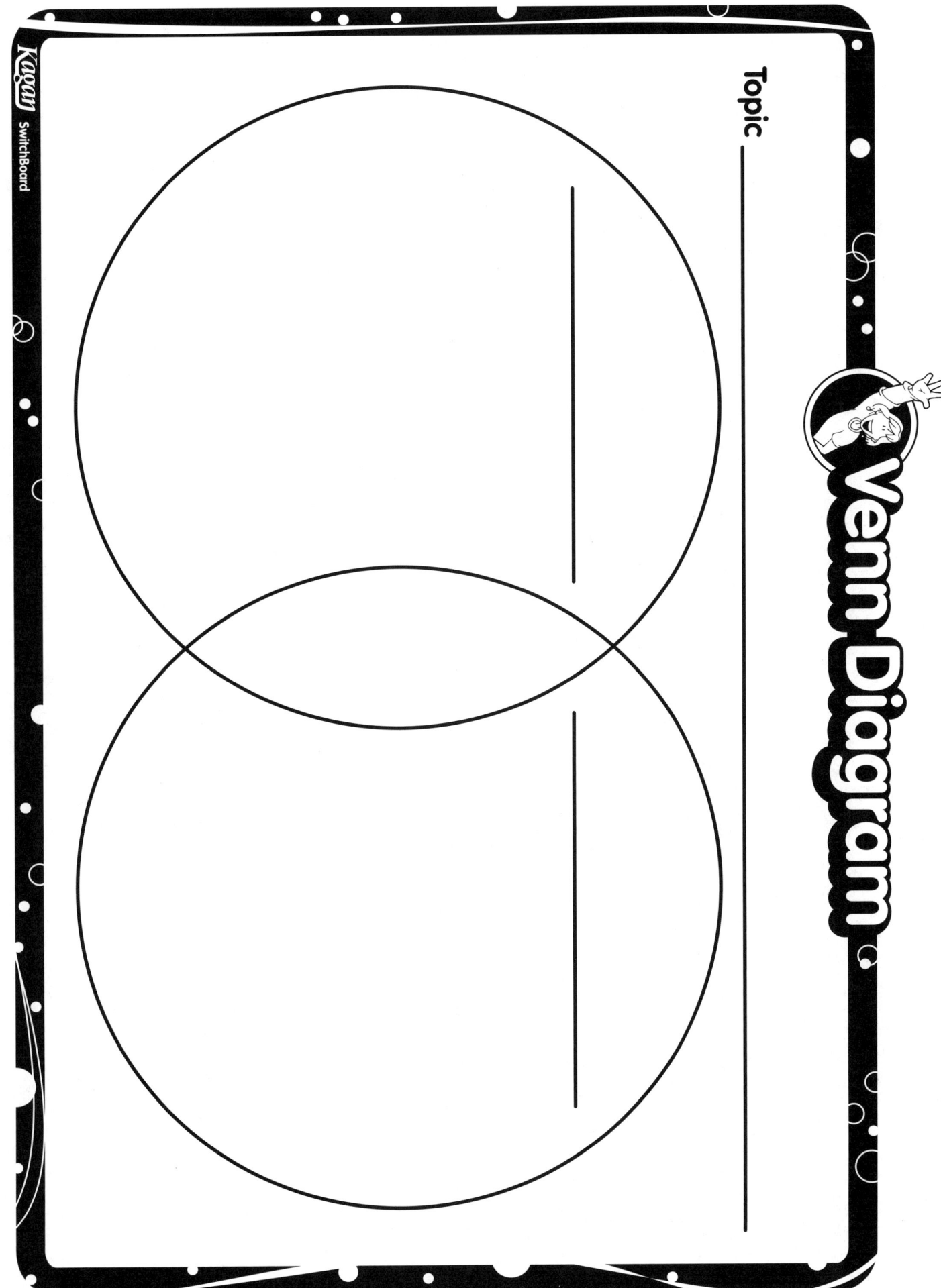

Word and Definition

Word	Definition

Yes/No Chart

Topic _____	Yes!	No!

Mathematics

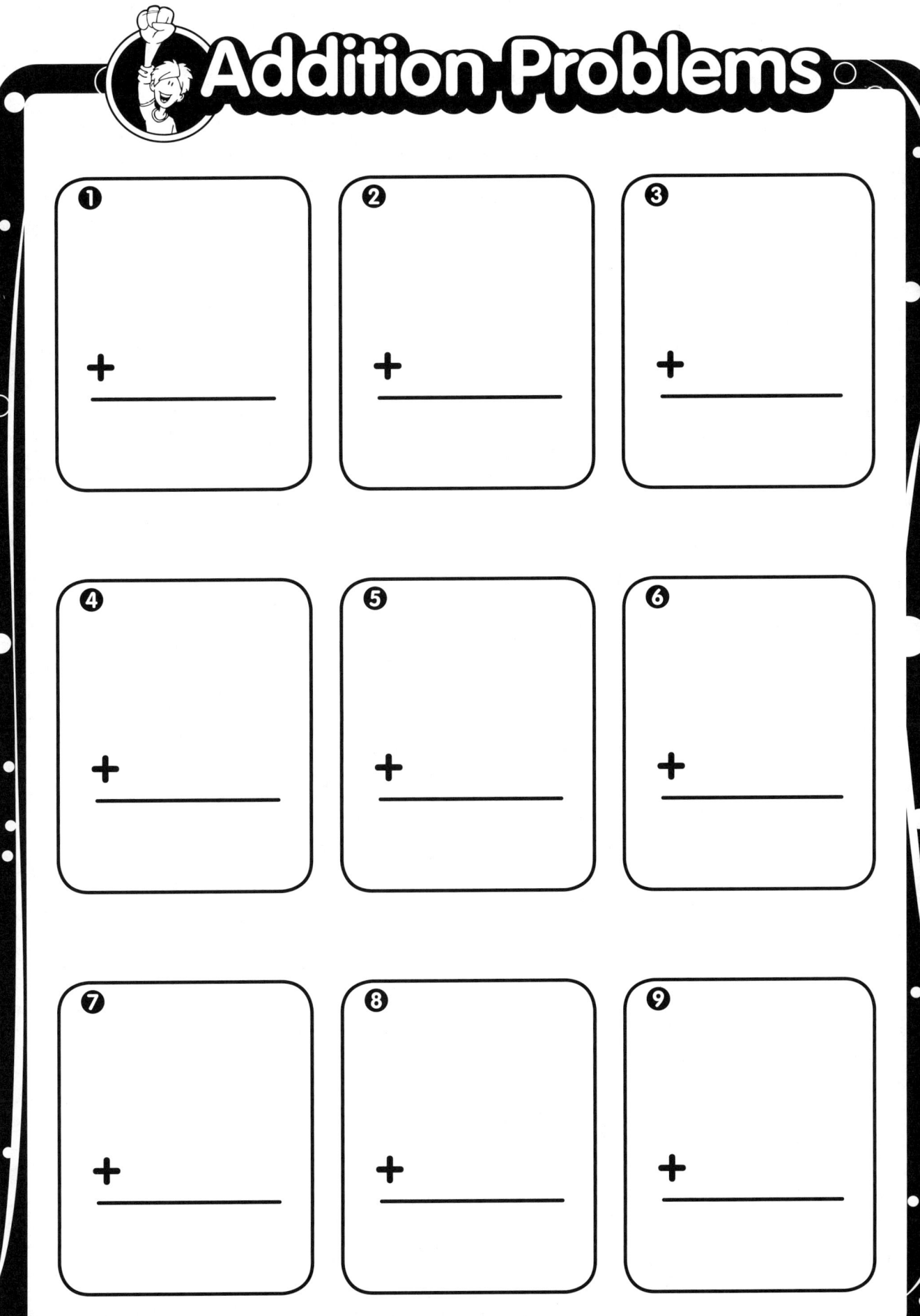

10			
9			
8			
7			
6			
5			
4			
3			
2			
1			
0			
	Item 1	Item 2	Item 3

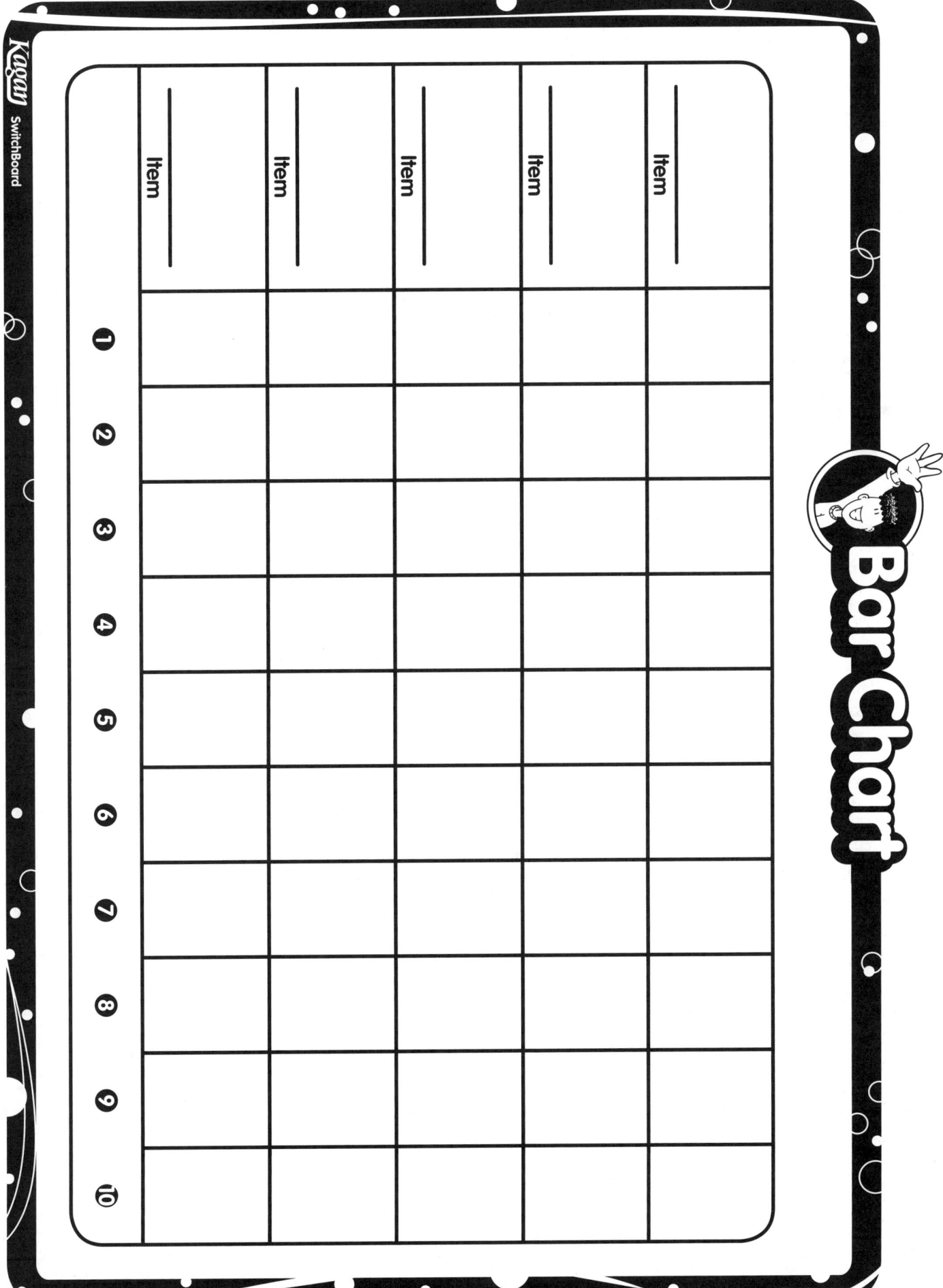

Bar Graph Template

Topic _____

Base 10

Hundreds

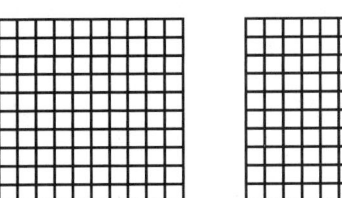 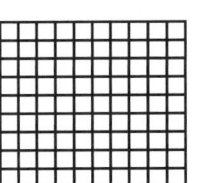 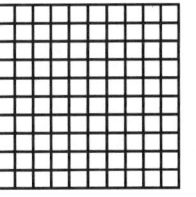 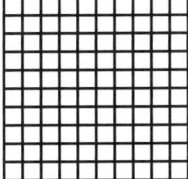

Tens

Ones

Base 10 Grid Paper

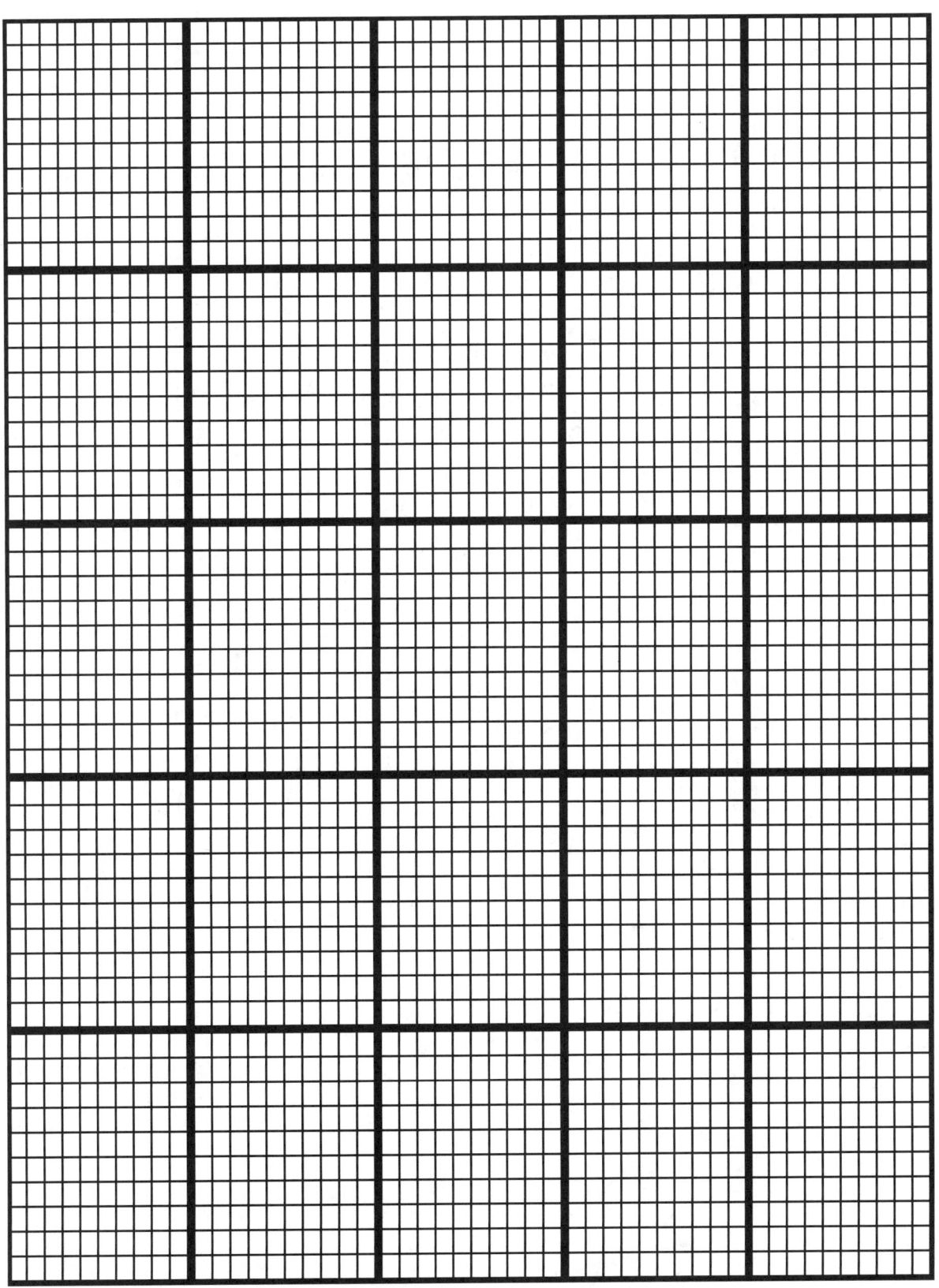

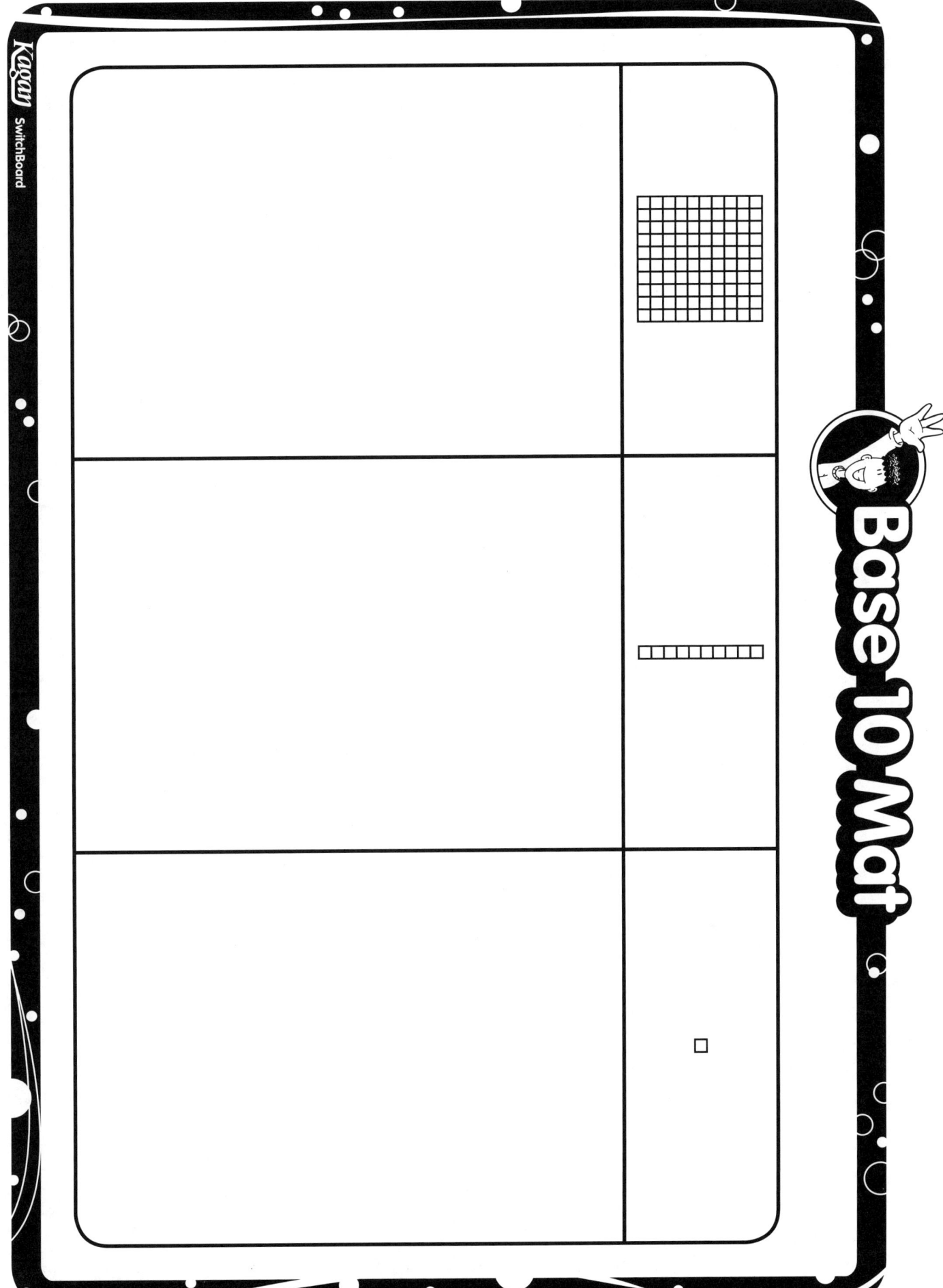

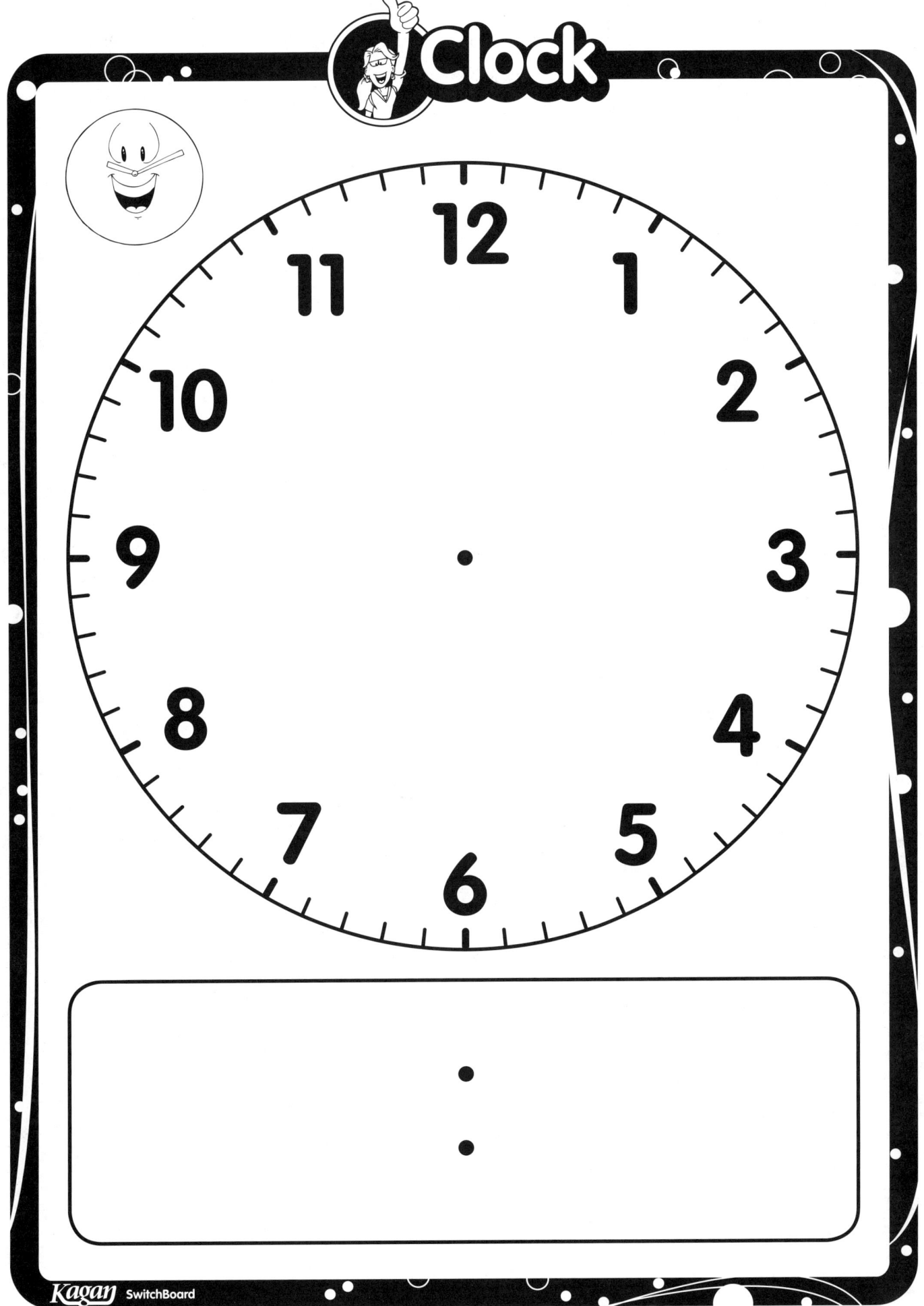

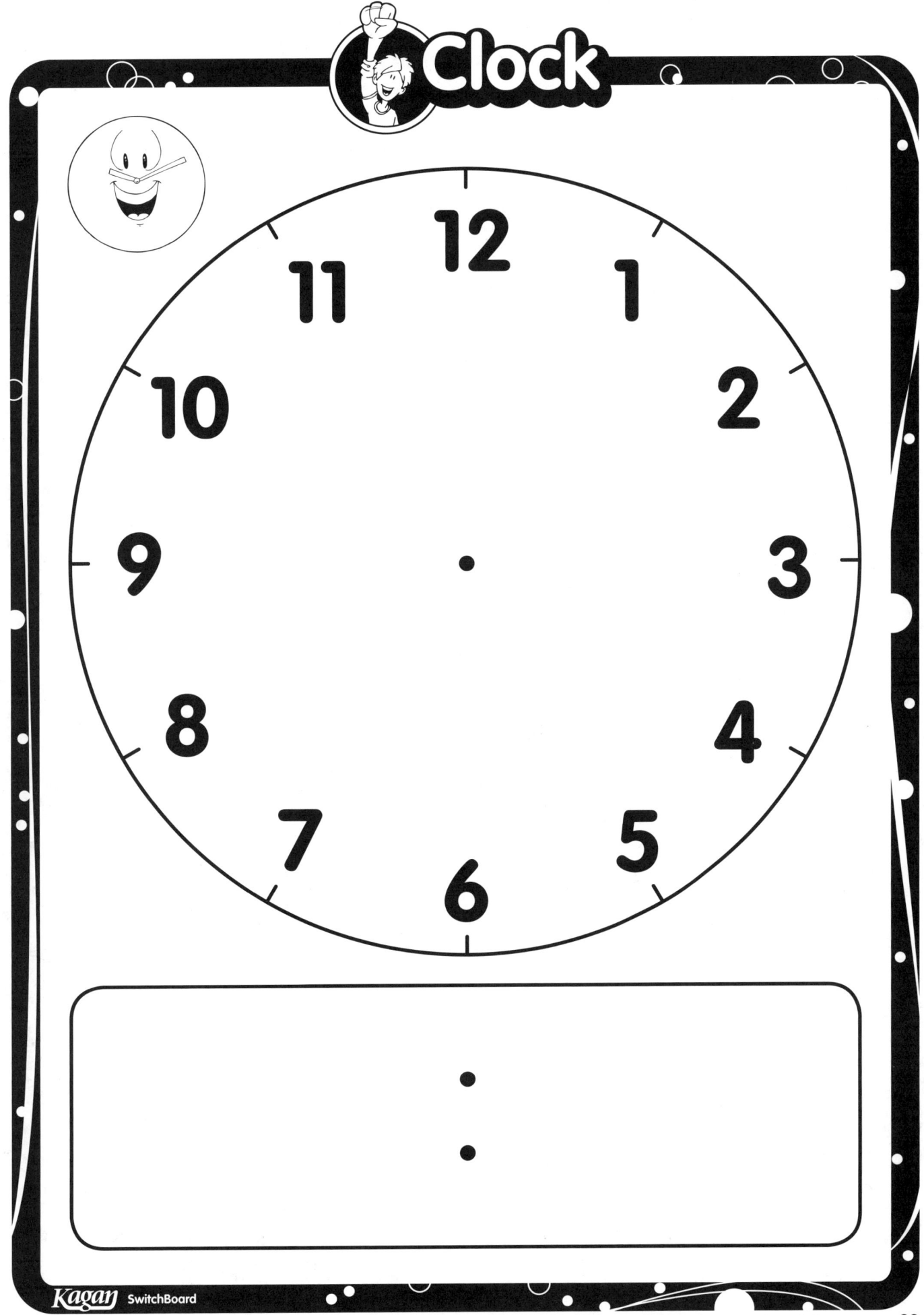

$

Coordinate Grid 10x10

Division Problems

① ② ③

④ ⑤ ⑥

⑦ ⑧ ⑨

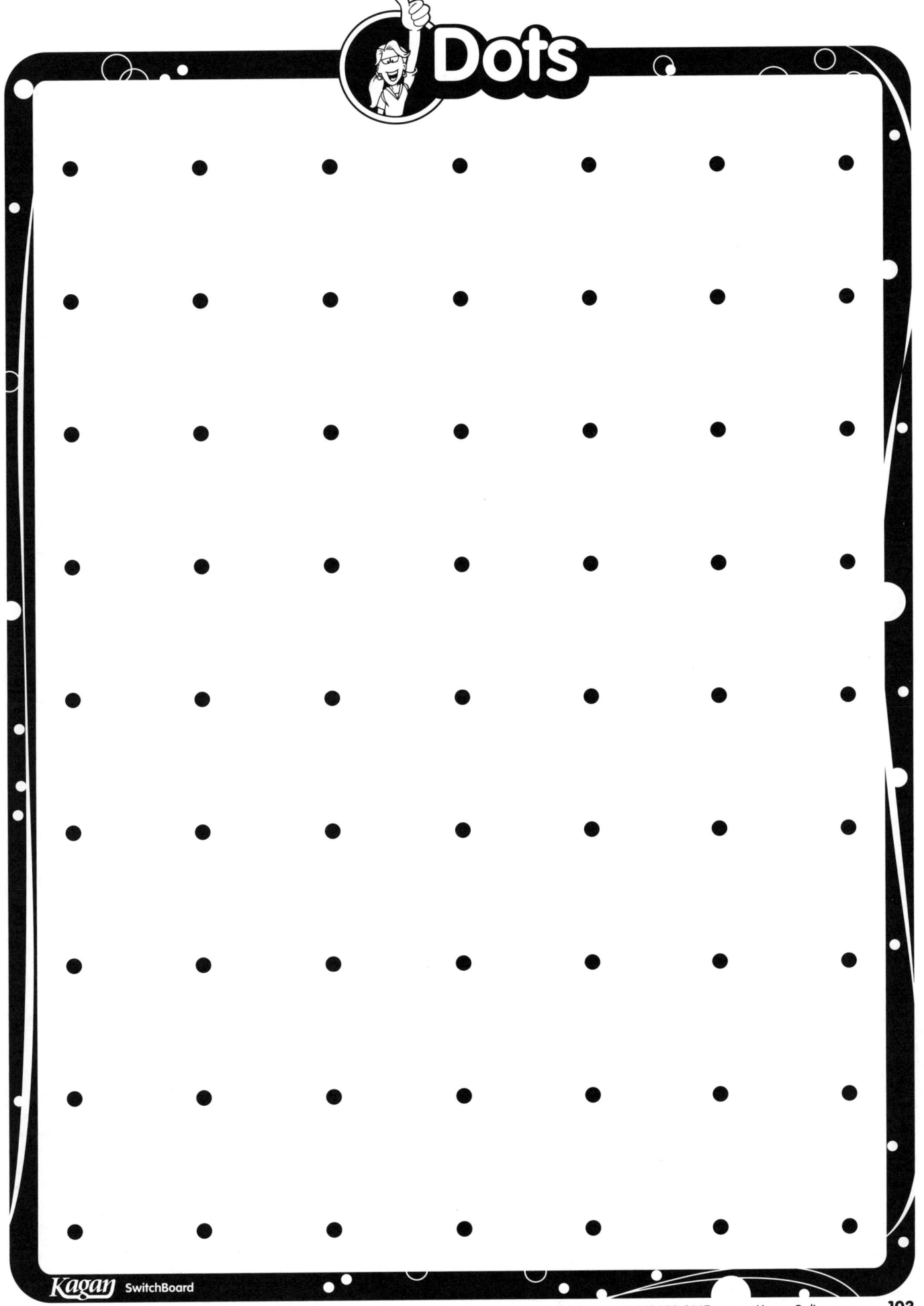

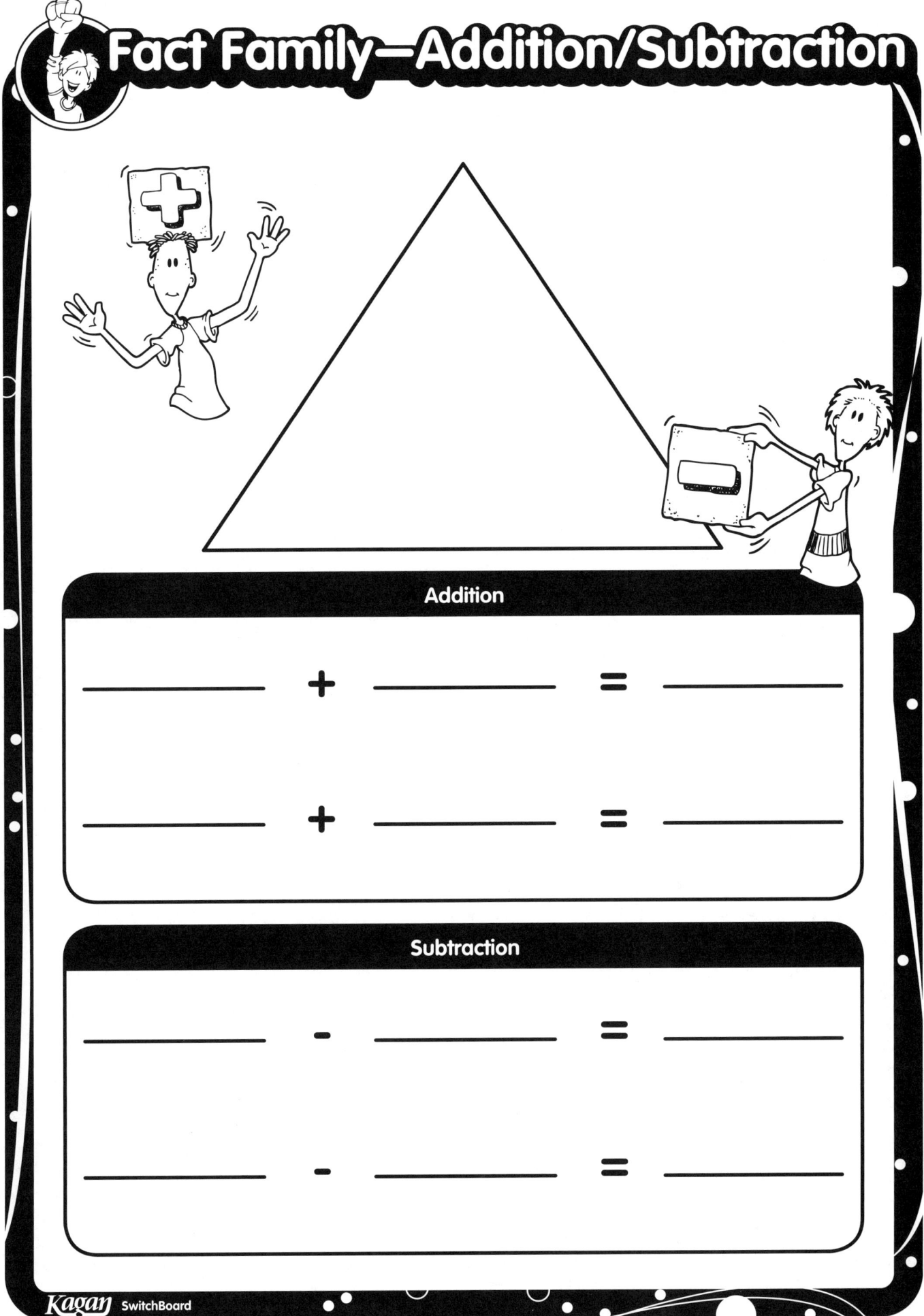

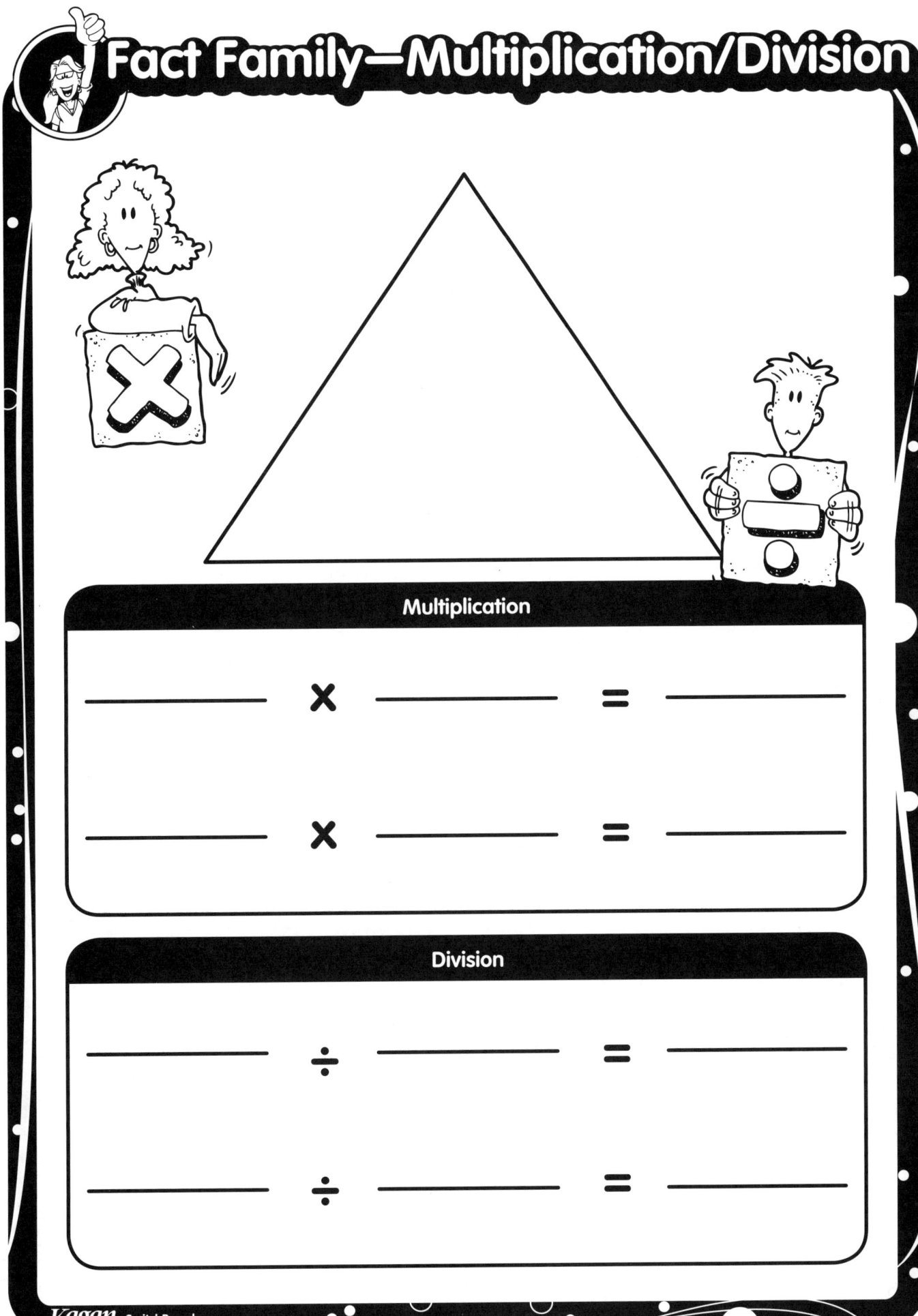

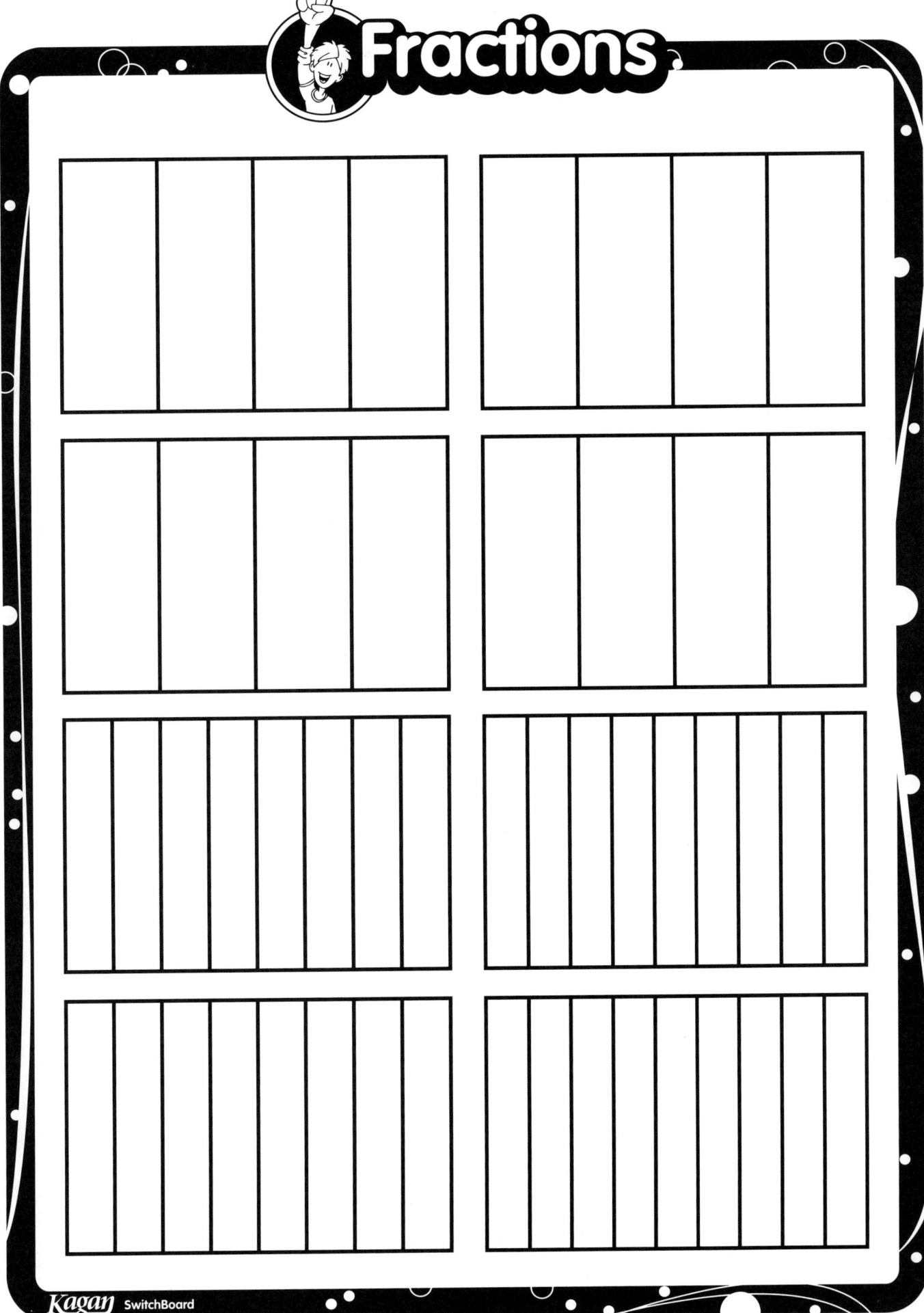

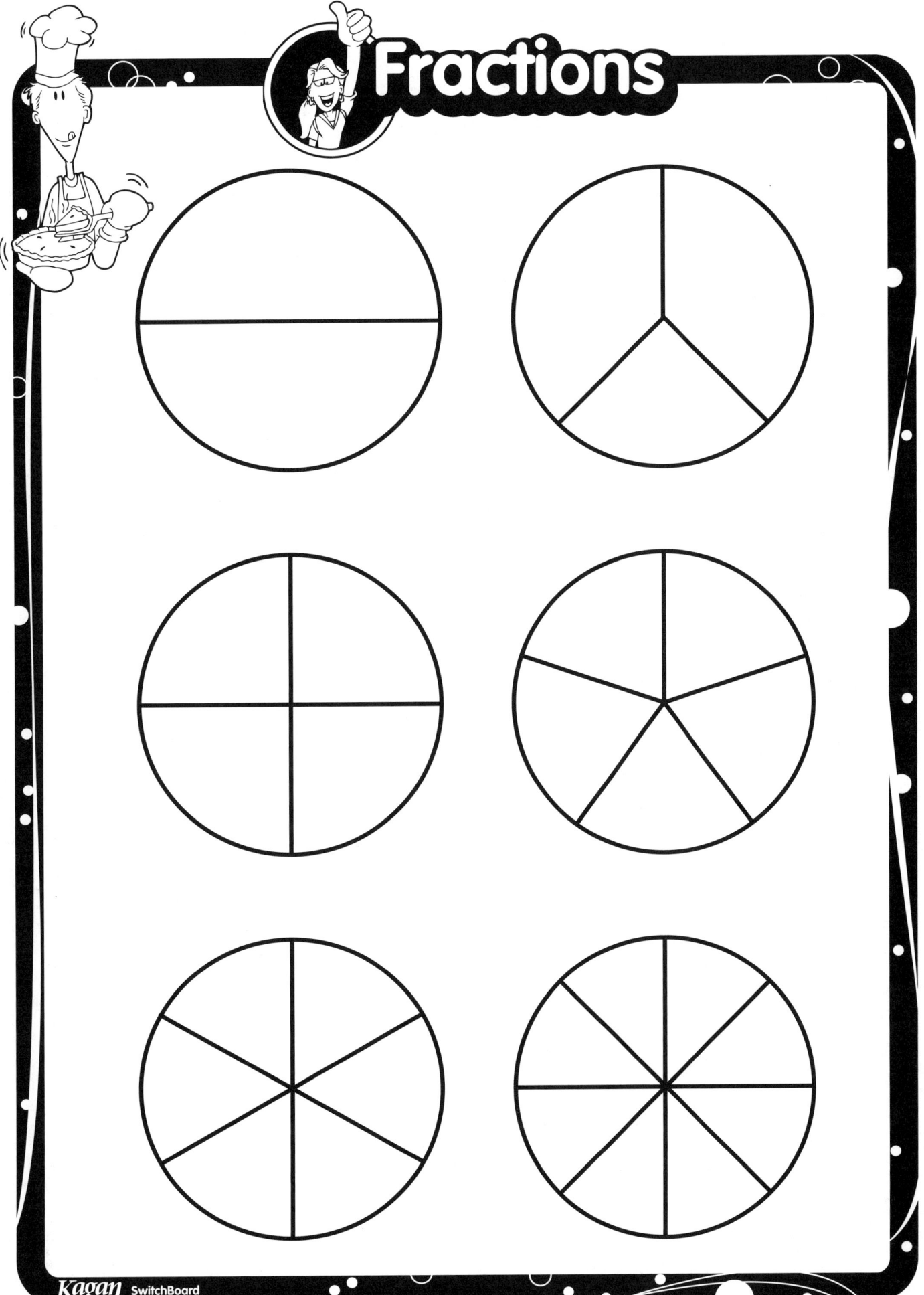

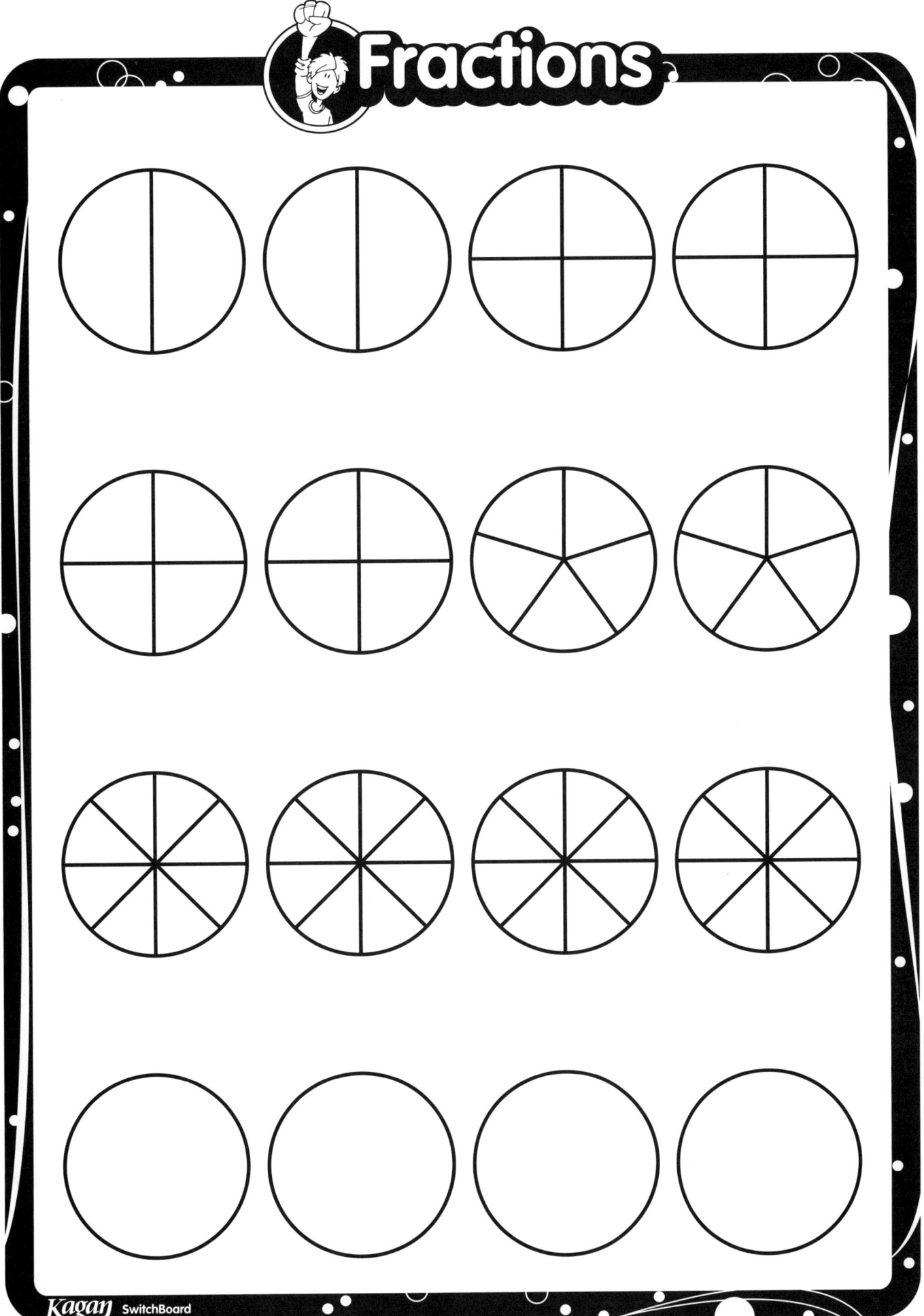

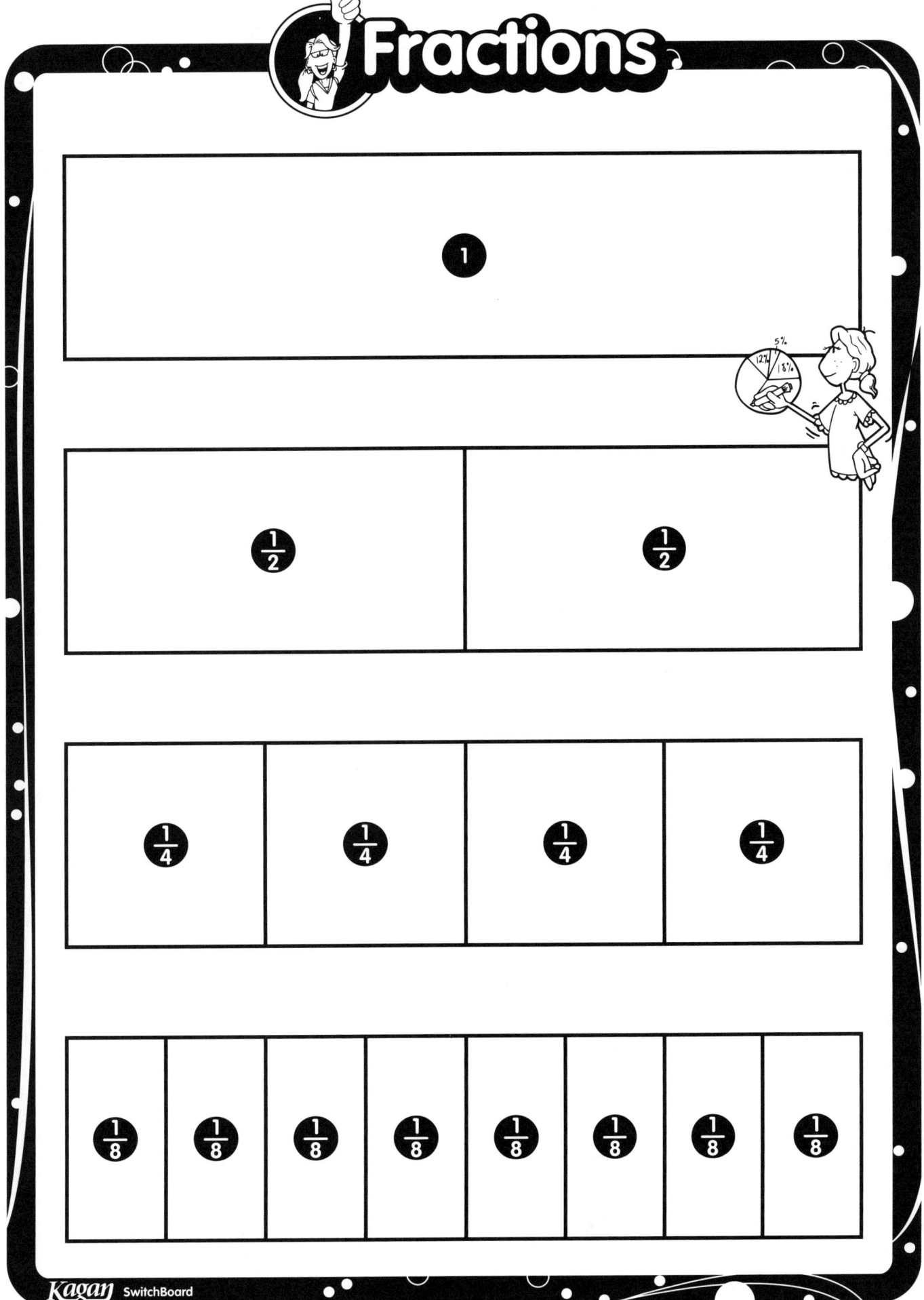

Graph Paper

Kagan SwitchBoard

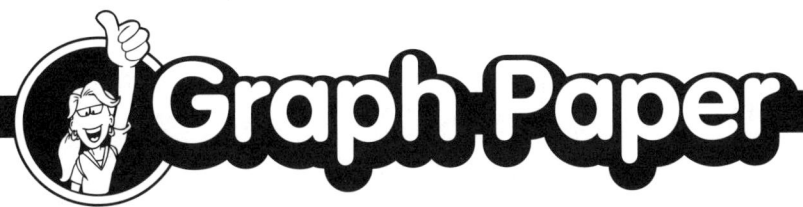

Greater Than, Less Than, Equal To

Hundred Number Chart

1	2	3	4	5	6	7	8	9	10
11	12	13	14	15	16	17	18	19	20
21	22	23	24	25	26	27	28	29	30
31	32	33	34	35	36	37	38	39	40
41	42	43	44	45	46	47	48	49	50
51	52	53	54	55	56	57	58	59	60
61	62	63	64	65	66	67	68	69	70
71	72	73	74	75	76	77	78	79	80
81	82	83	84	85	86	87	88	89	90
91	92	93	94	95	96	97	98	99	100

Isometric Dot Pattern

Multiplication Array

	1	2	3	4	5	6	7	8	9	10
1										
2										
3										
4										
5										
6										
7										
8										
9										
10										

Multiplication Mat 1-9

X	1	2	3	4	5	6	7	8	9
1	1	2	3	4	5	6	7	8	9
2	2	4	6	8	10	12	14	16	18
3	3	6	9	12	15	18	21	24	27
4	4	8	12	16	20	24	28	32	36
5	5	10	15	20	25	30	35	40	45
6	6	12	18	24	30	36	42	48	54
7	7	14	21	28	35	42	49	56	63
8	8	16	24	32	40	48	56	64	72
9	9	18	27	36	45	54	63	80	81

Multiplication Mat 1-12

X	1	2	3	4	5	6	7	8	9	10	11	12
1	1	2	3	4	5	6	7	8	9	10	11	12
2	2	4	6	8	10	12	14	16	18	20	22	24
3	3	6	9	12	15	18	21	24	27	30	33	36
4	4	8	12	16	20	24	28	32	36	40	44	48
5	5	10	15	20	25	30	35	40	45	50	55	60
6	6	12	18	24	30	36	42	48	54	60	66	72
7	7	14	21	28	35	42	49	56	63	70	77	84
8	8	16	24	32	40	48	56	64	72	80	88	96
9	9	18	27	36	46	54	63	72	81	90	99	108
10	19	20	30	40	50	60	70	80	90	100	110	120
11	11	22	33	44	55	66	77	88	99	110	121	132
12	12	24	36	48	60	72	84	96	108	120	132	144

Kagan SwitchBoard

SwitchBoard Templates • Kagan Publishing • 1 (800) 933-2667 • www.KaganOnline.com

Multiplication Problems

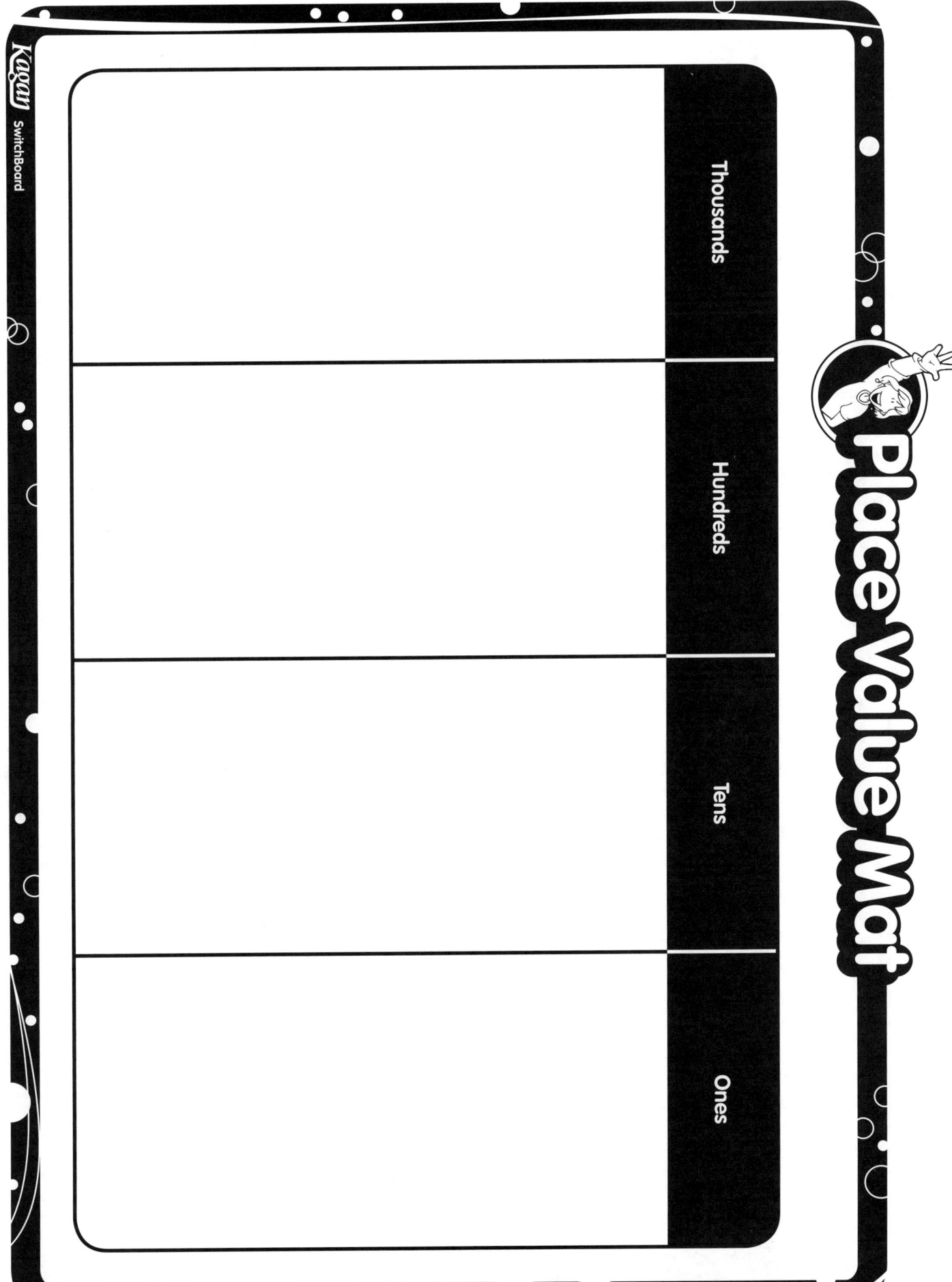

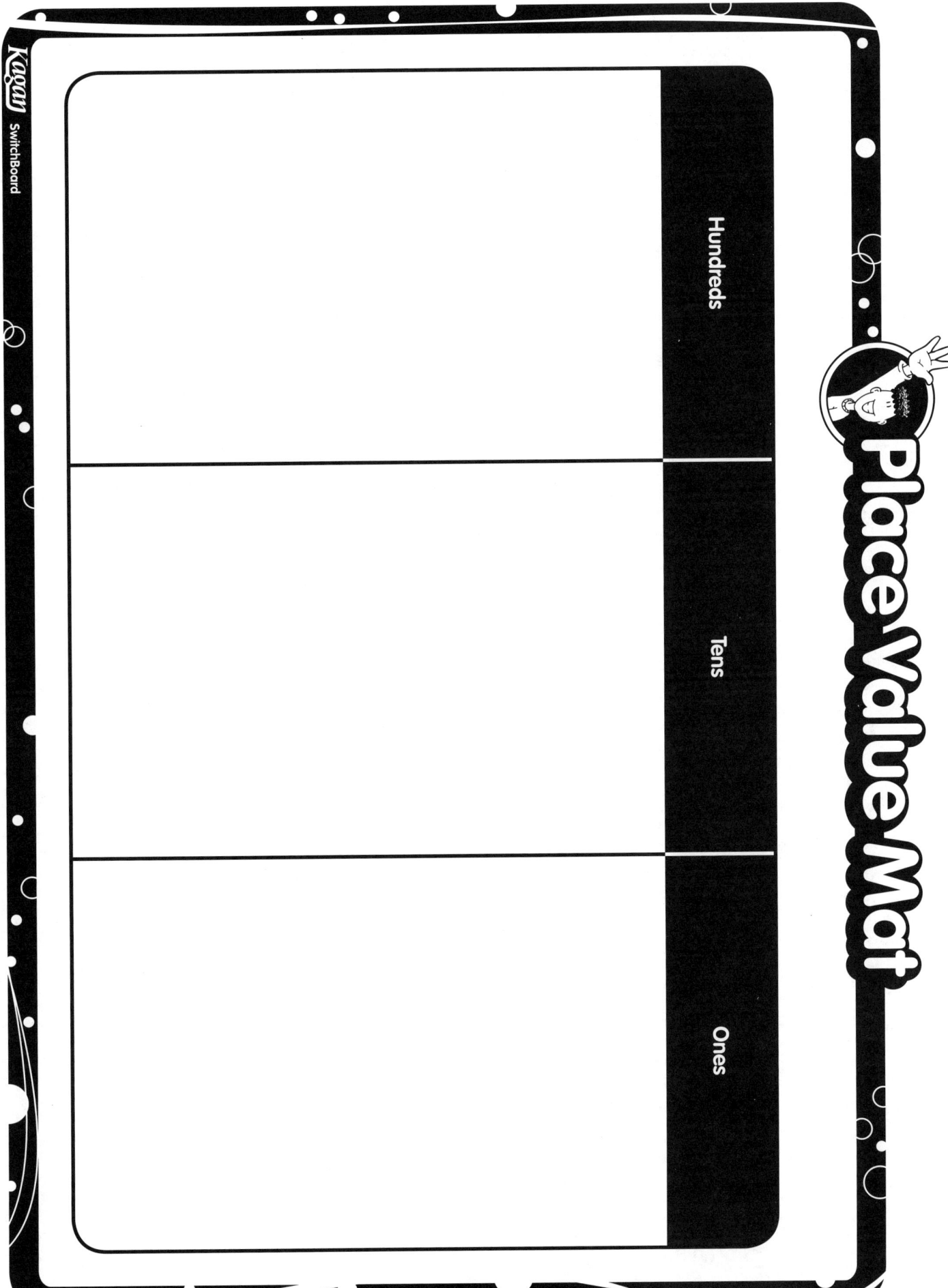

Place Value Mat—Decimals

	Hundreds
	Tens
	Ones
	Tenths
	Hundredths
	Thousandths

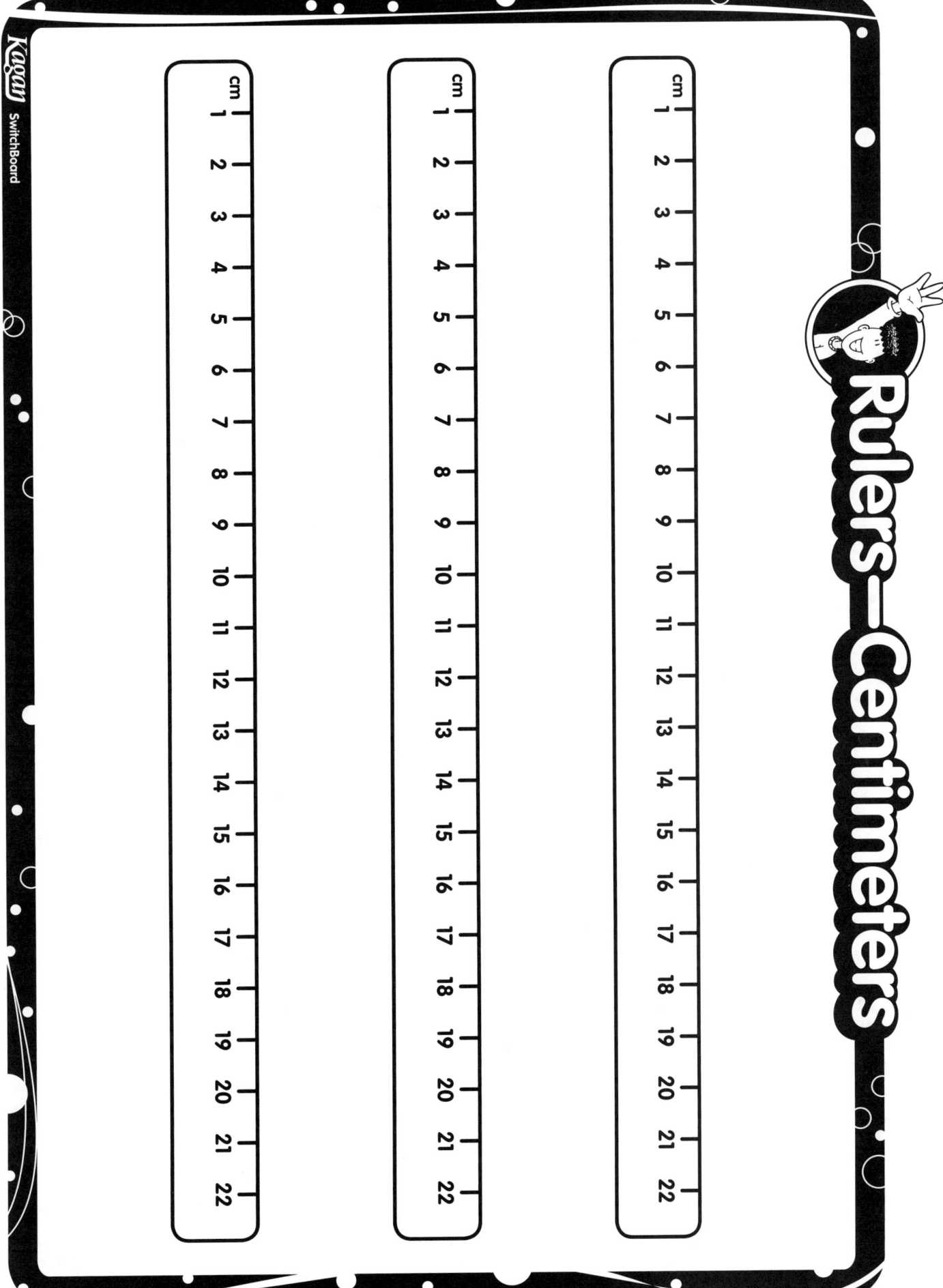

Rulers—Centimeters

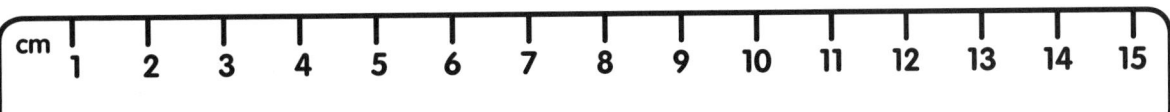

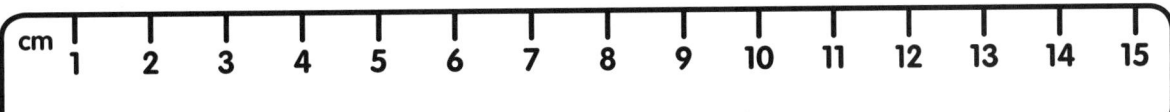

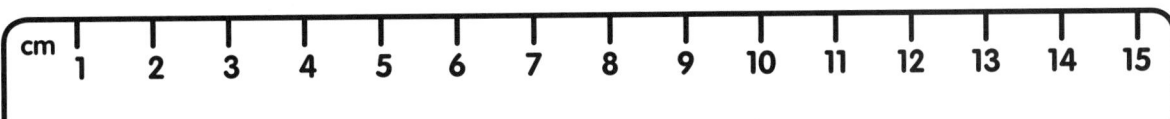

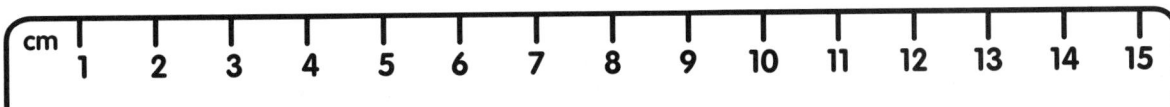

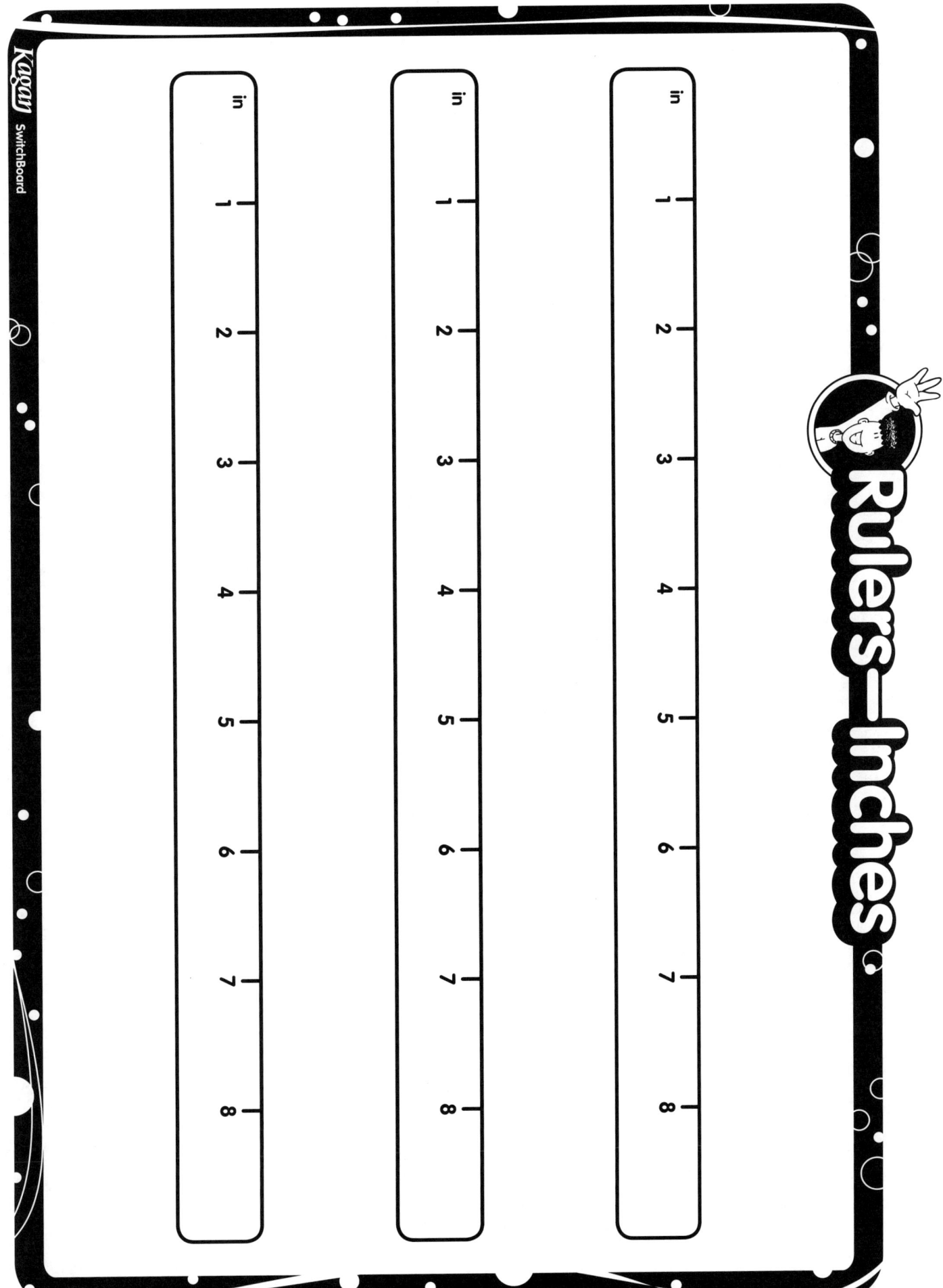

Rulers—Inches

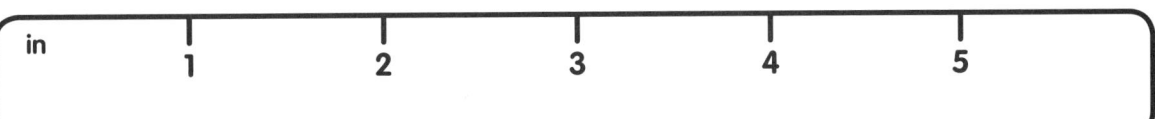

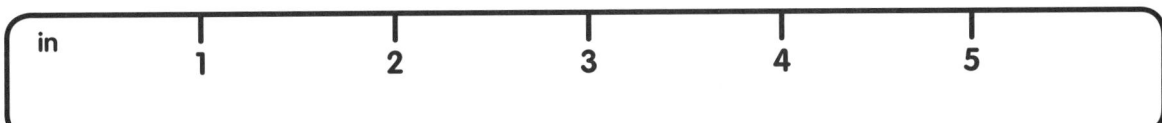

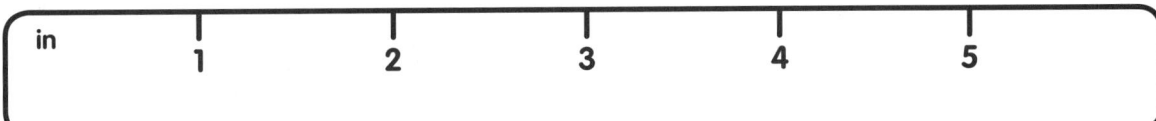

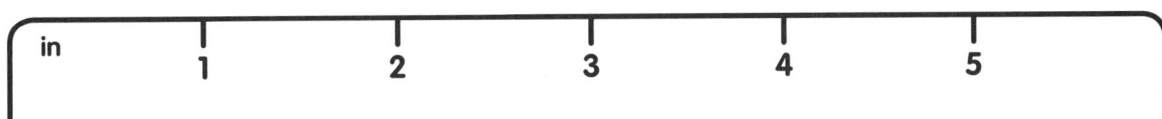

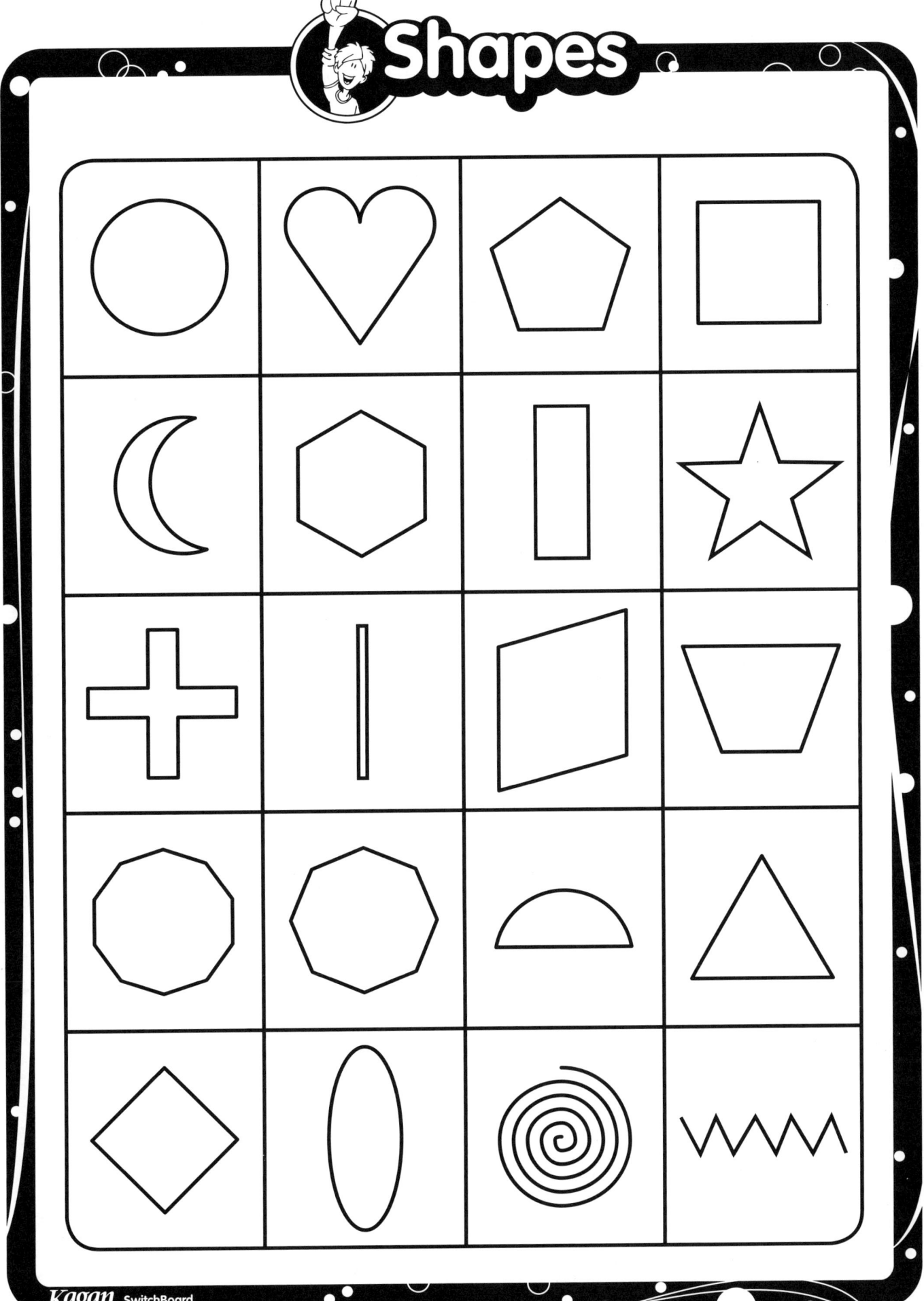

Subtraction Problems

①

②

③

④

⑤

⑥

⑦

⑧

⑨

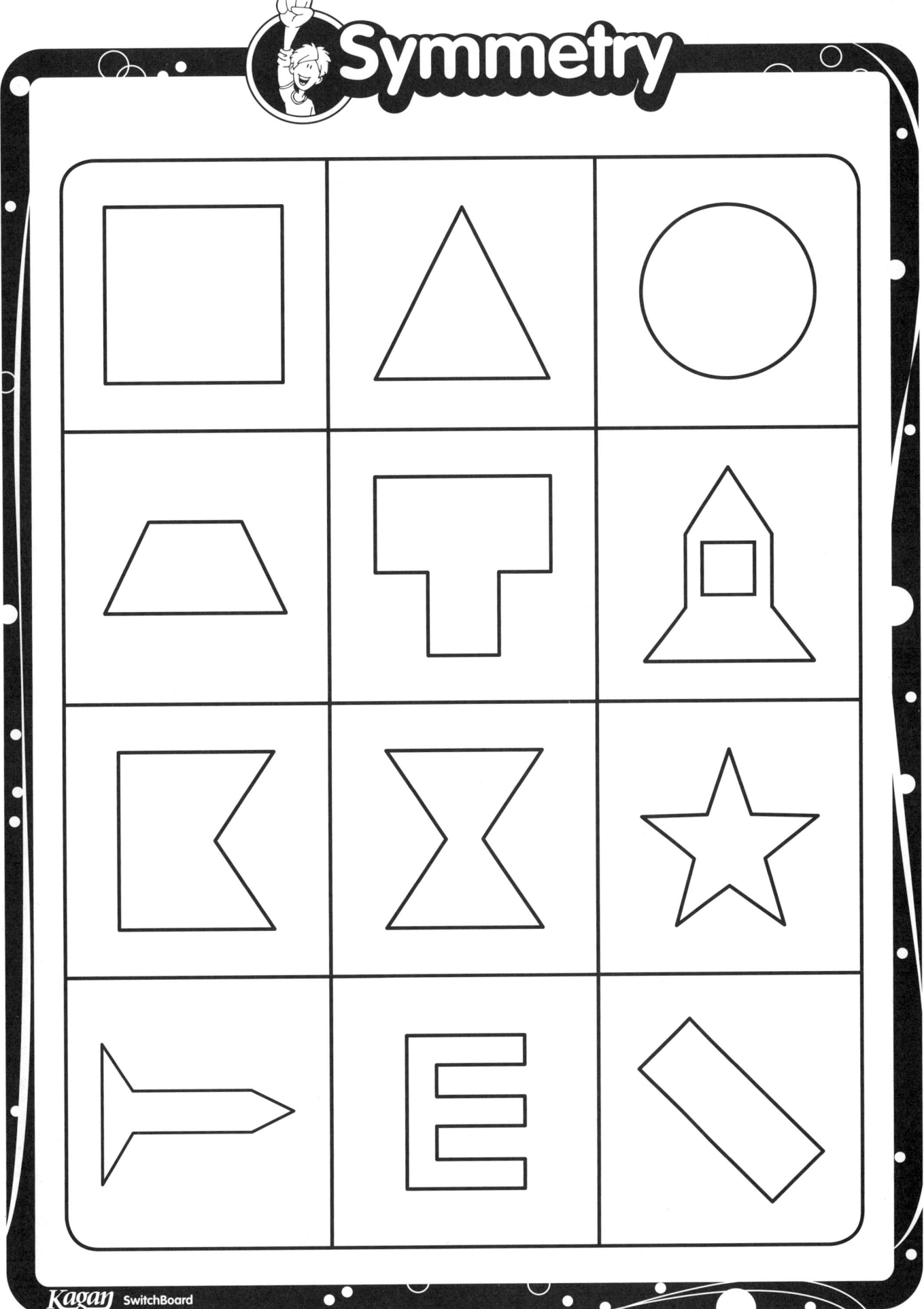

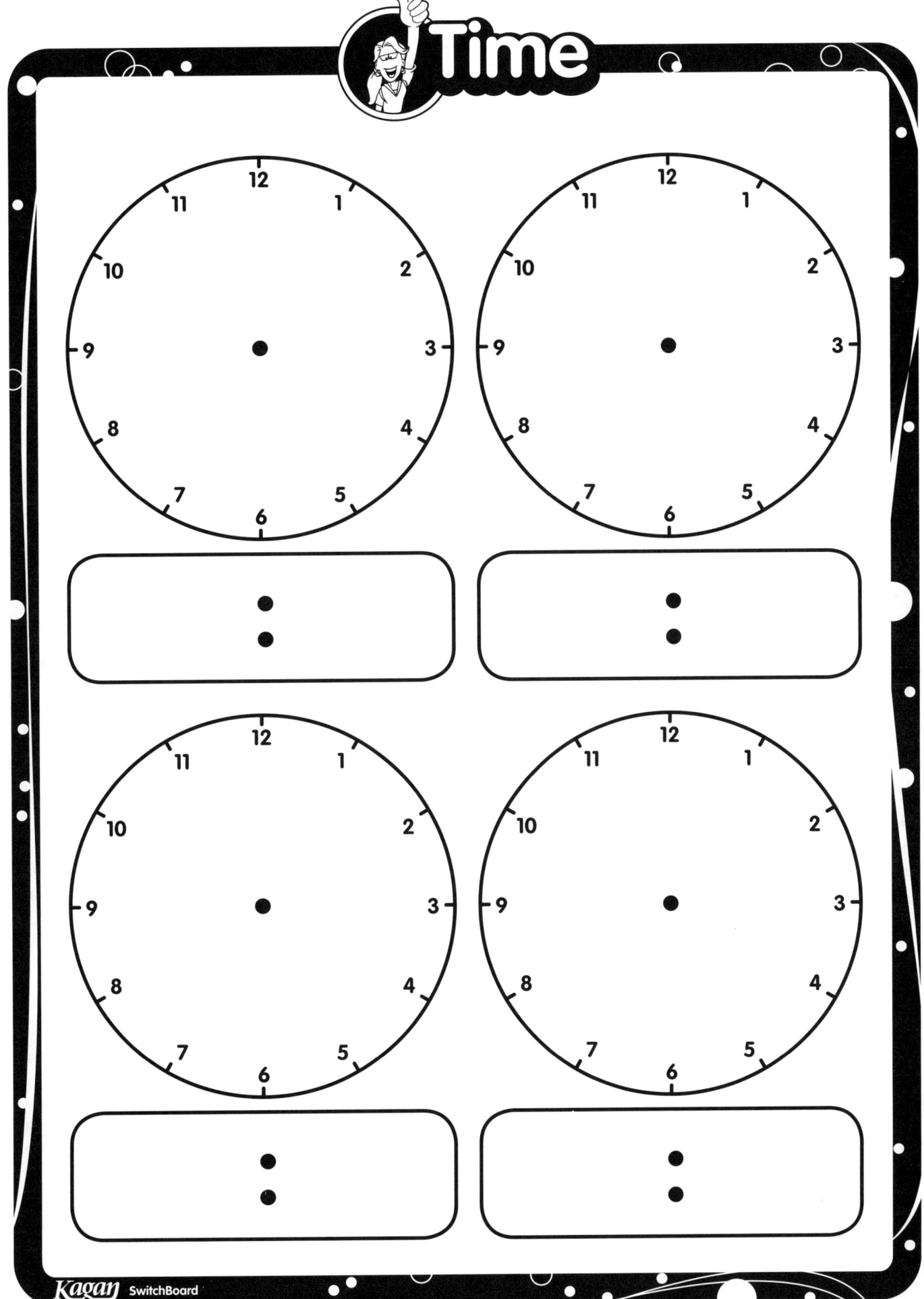

Triangle Fact Family

Language Arts

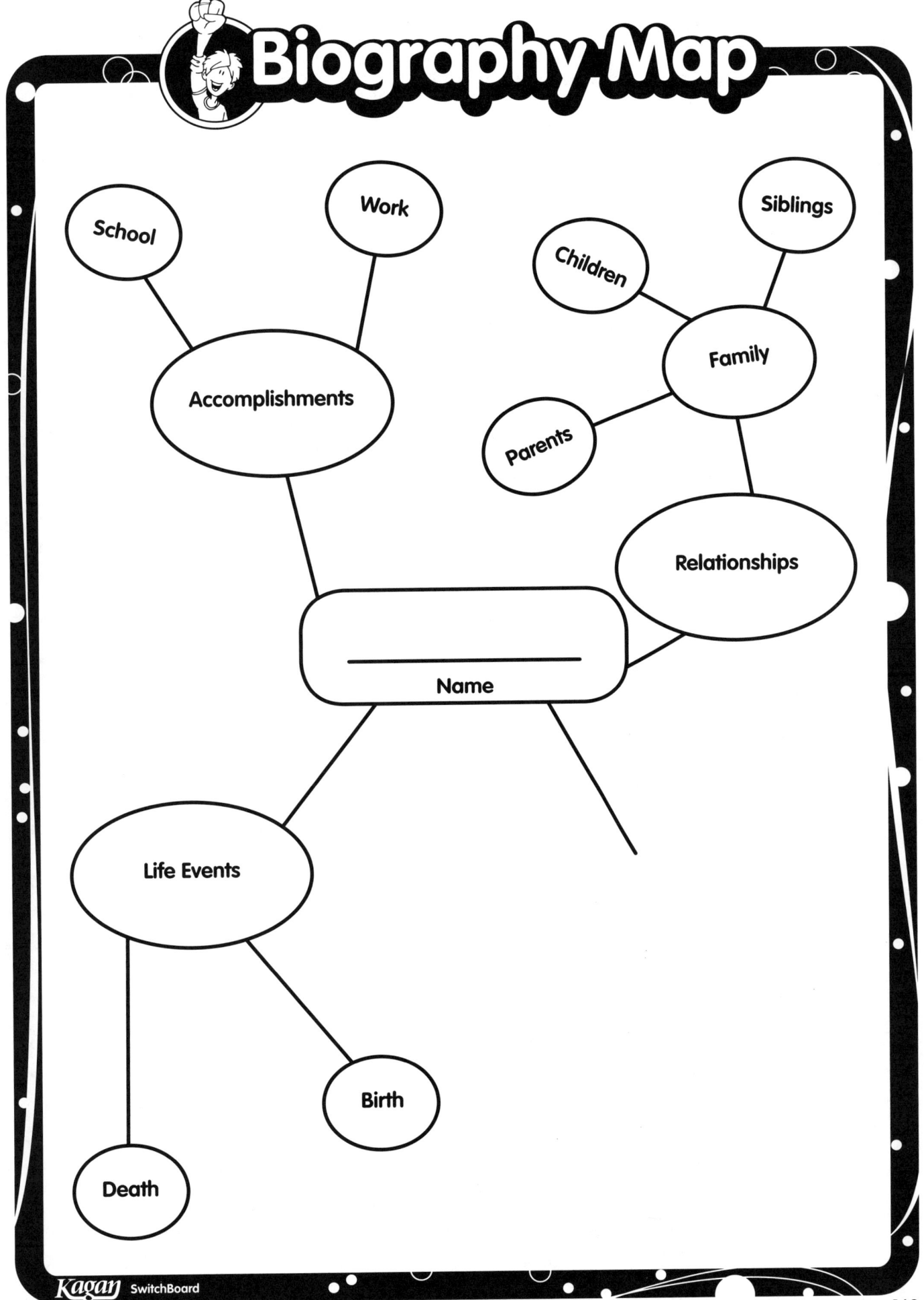

Biography Star Chart

Name _____

- Fact 1
- Fact 2
- Fact 3
- Fact 4
- Fact 5

Character Chart

	Looks	Says	Does
Character 1			
Character 2			
Character 3			

Character Chart

	Character 1	Character 2	Character 3	Character 4	Character 5
Appearance					
Actions					
Personality					
Relationships					
Says					

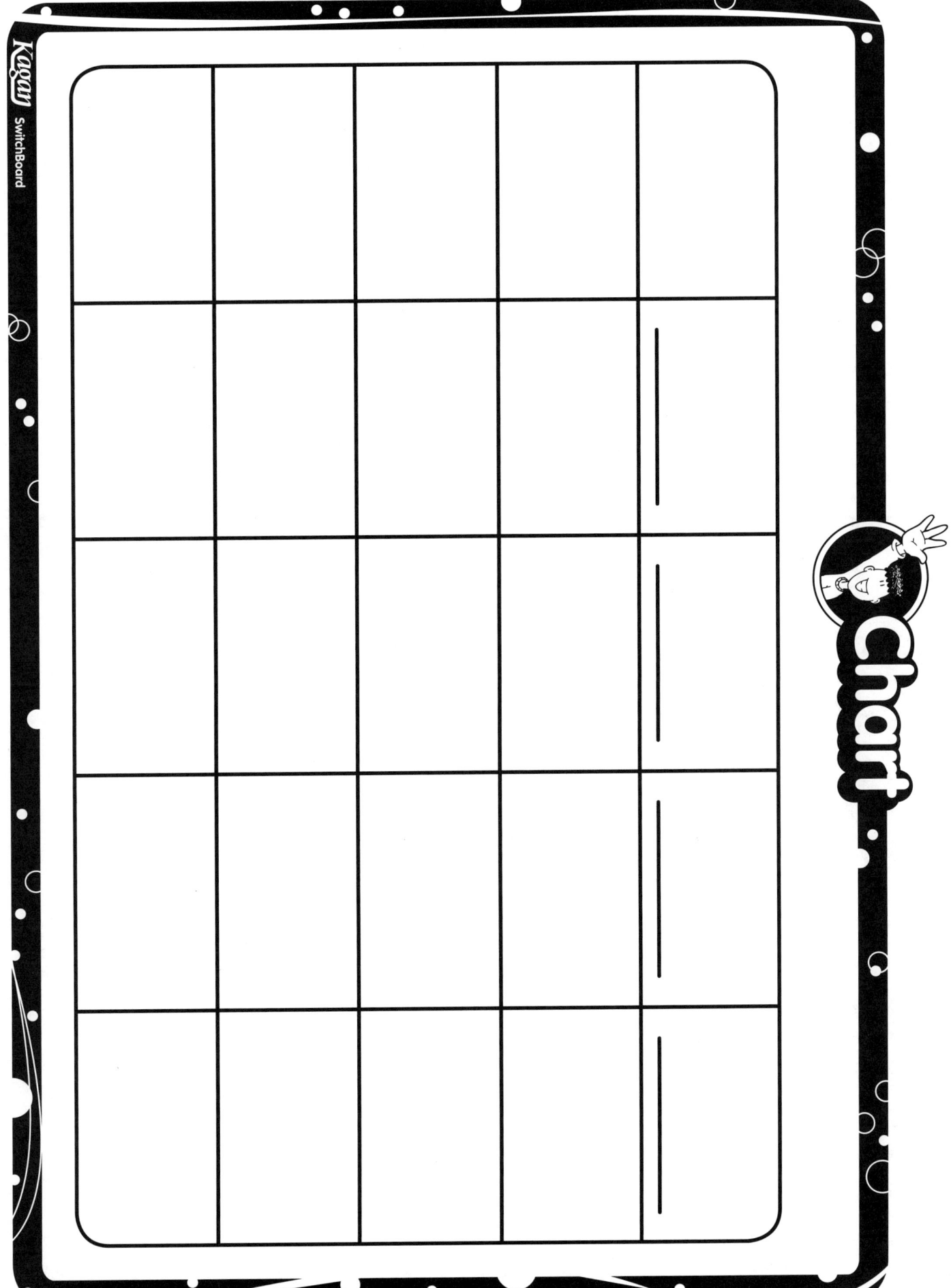

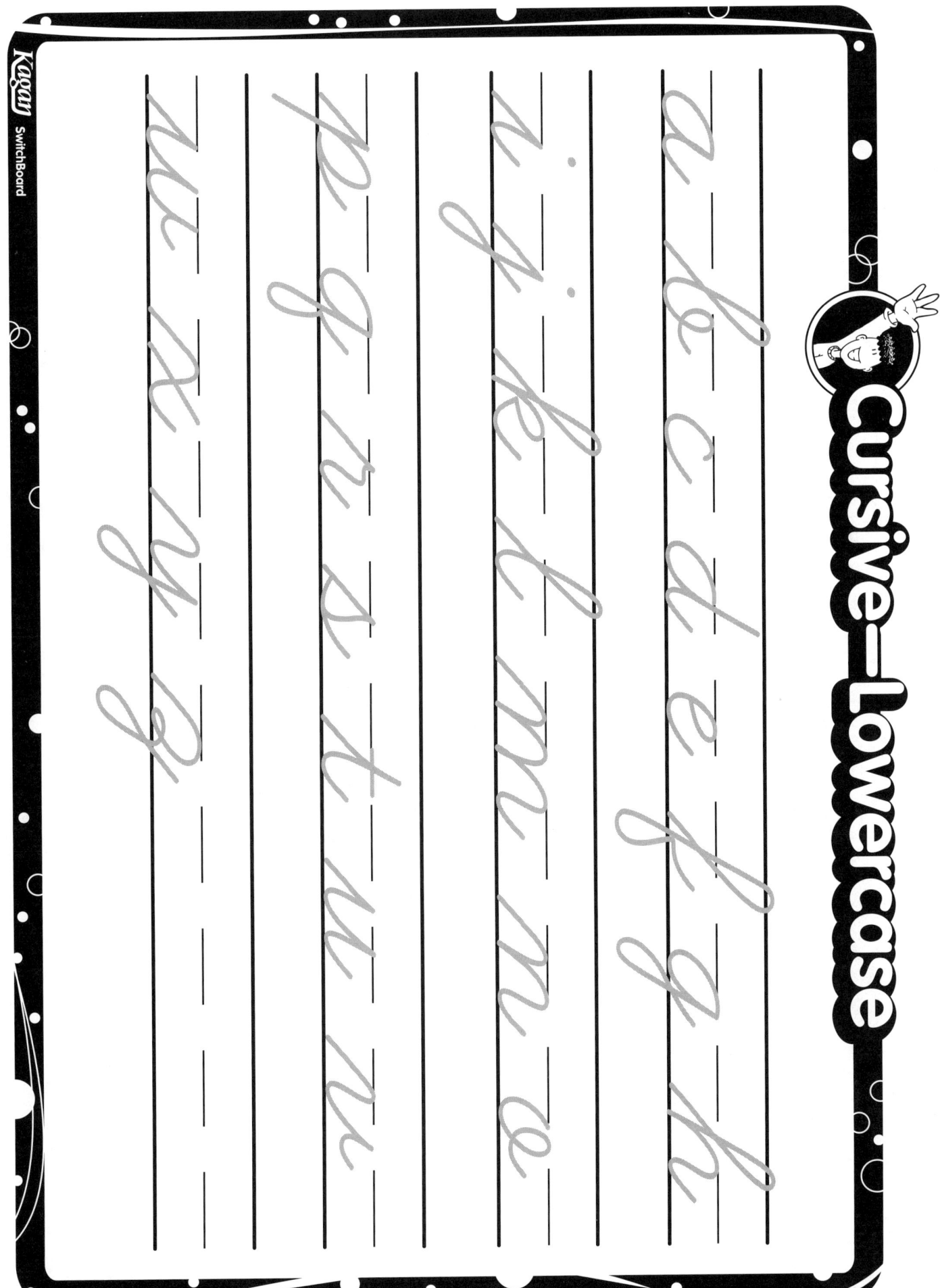

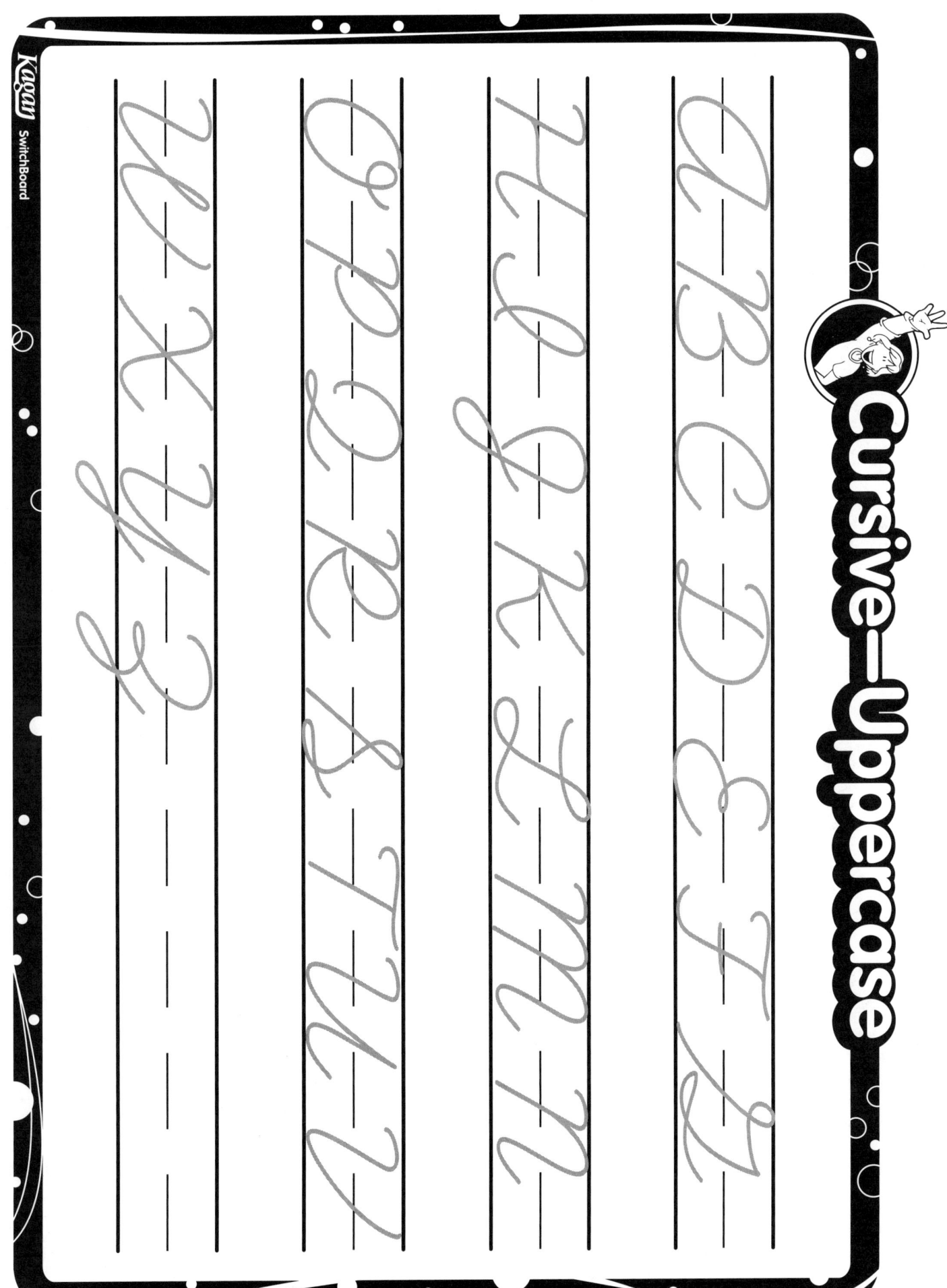

Descriptive Writing Star

Describe _____

★ Looks like…

★ Sounds like…

★ Tastes like…

★ Feels like…

★ Smells like…

Prompt

Response

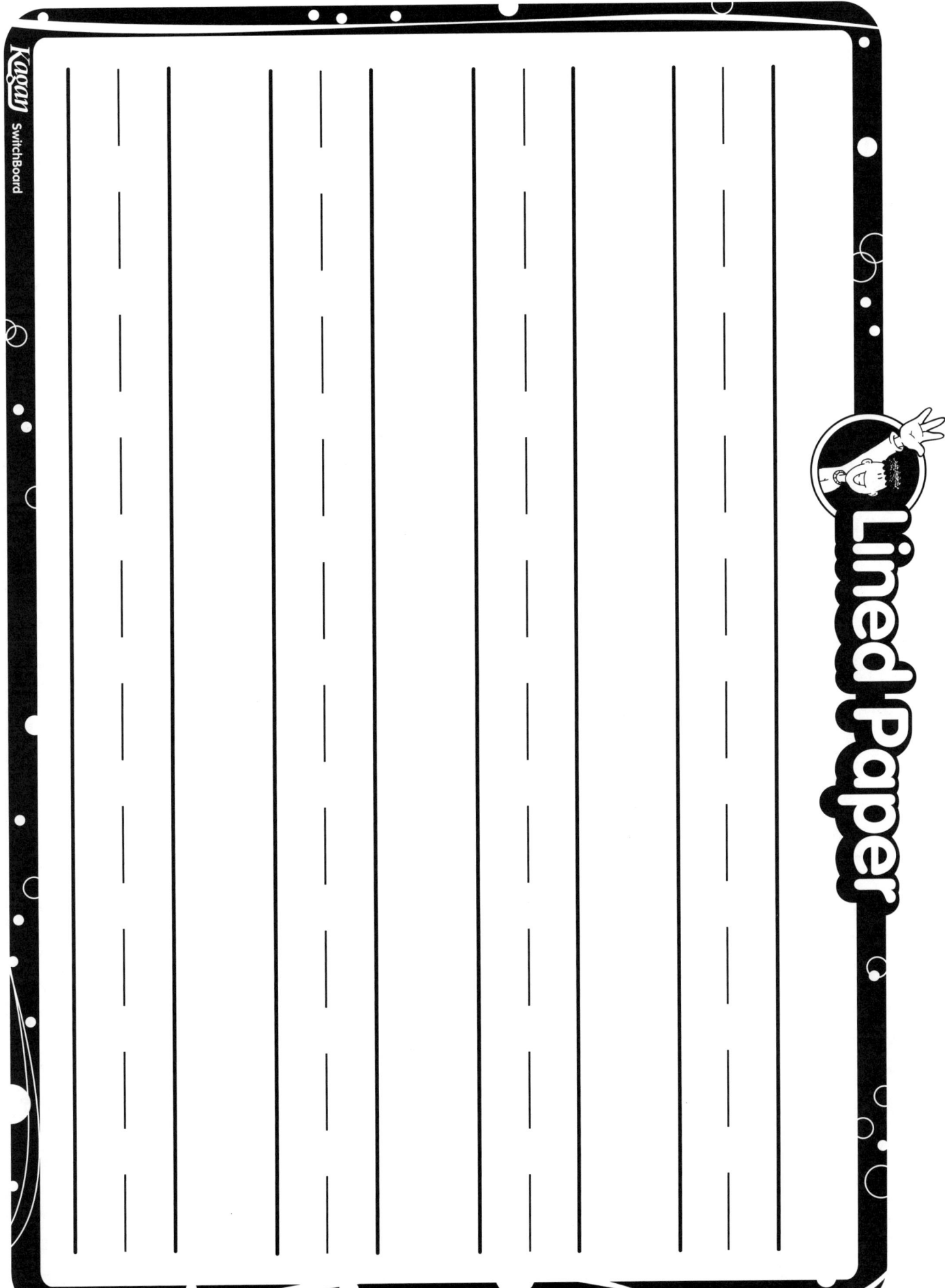

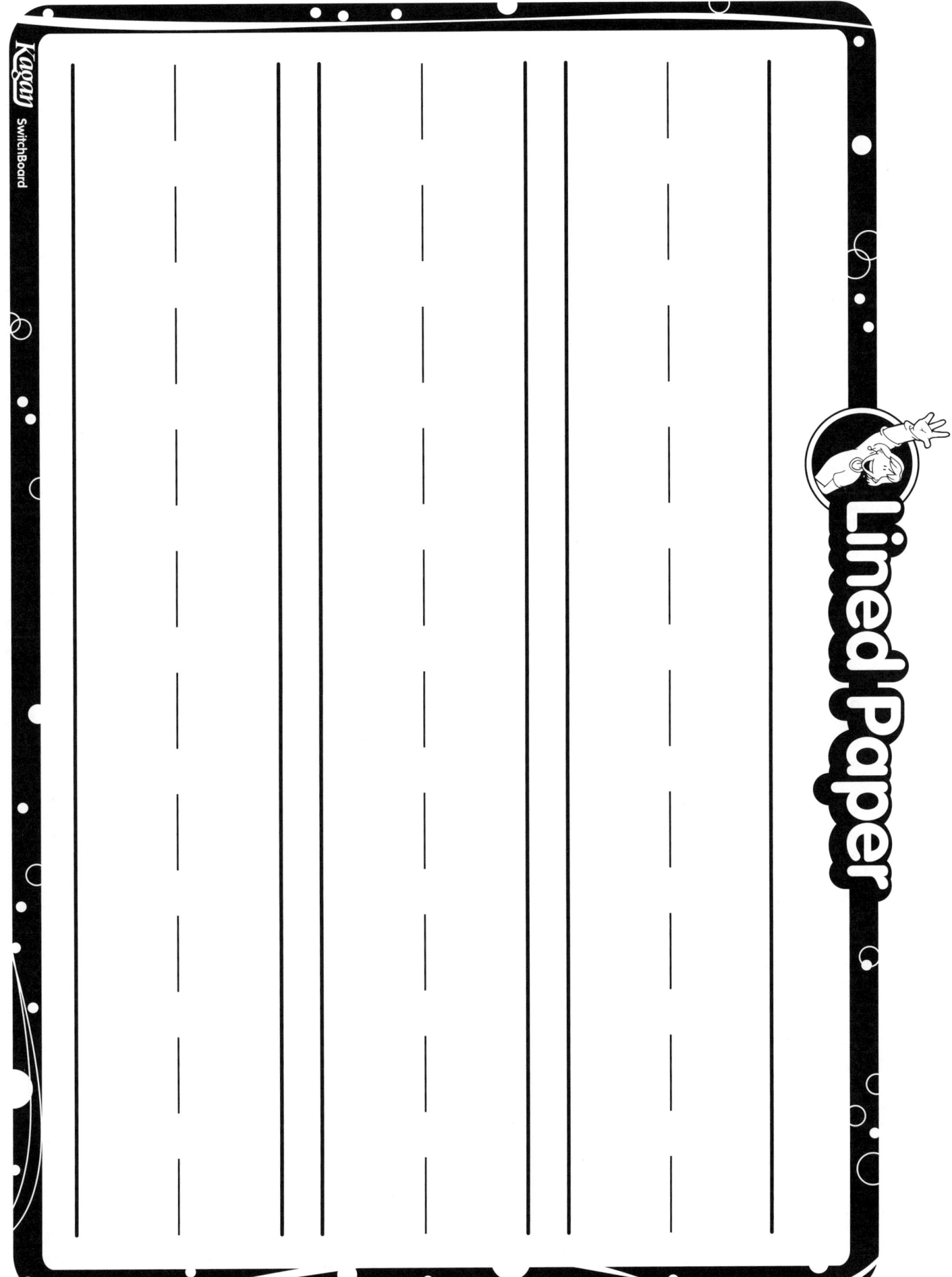

Outline

I. _____
   A. _____
      1. _____
      2. _____
      3. _____
   B. _____
      1. _____
      2. _____
      3. _____
   C. _____
      1. _____
      2. _____
      3. _____

II. _____
   A. _____
      1. _____
      2. _____
      3. _____
   B. _____
      1. _____
      2. _____
      3. _____
   C. _____
      1. _____
      2. _____
      3. _____

I. _____

    A. _____

    B. _____

    C. _____

II. _____

    A. _____

    B. _____

    C. _____

III. _____

    A. _____

    B. _____

    C. _____

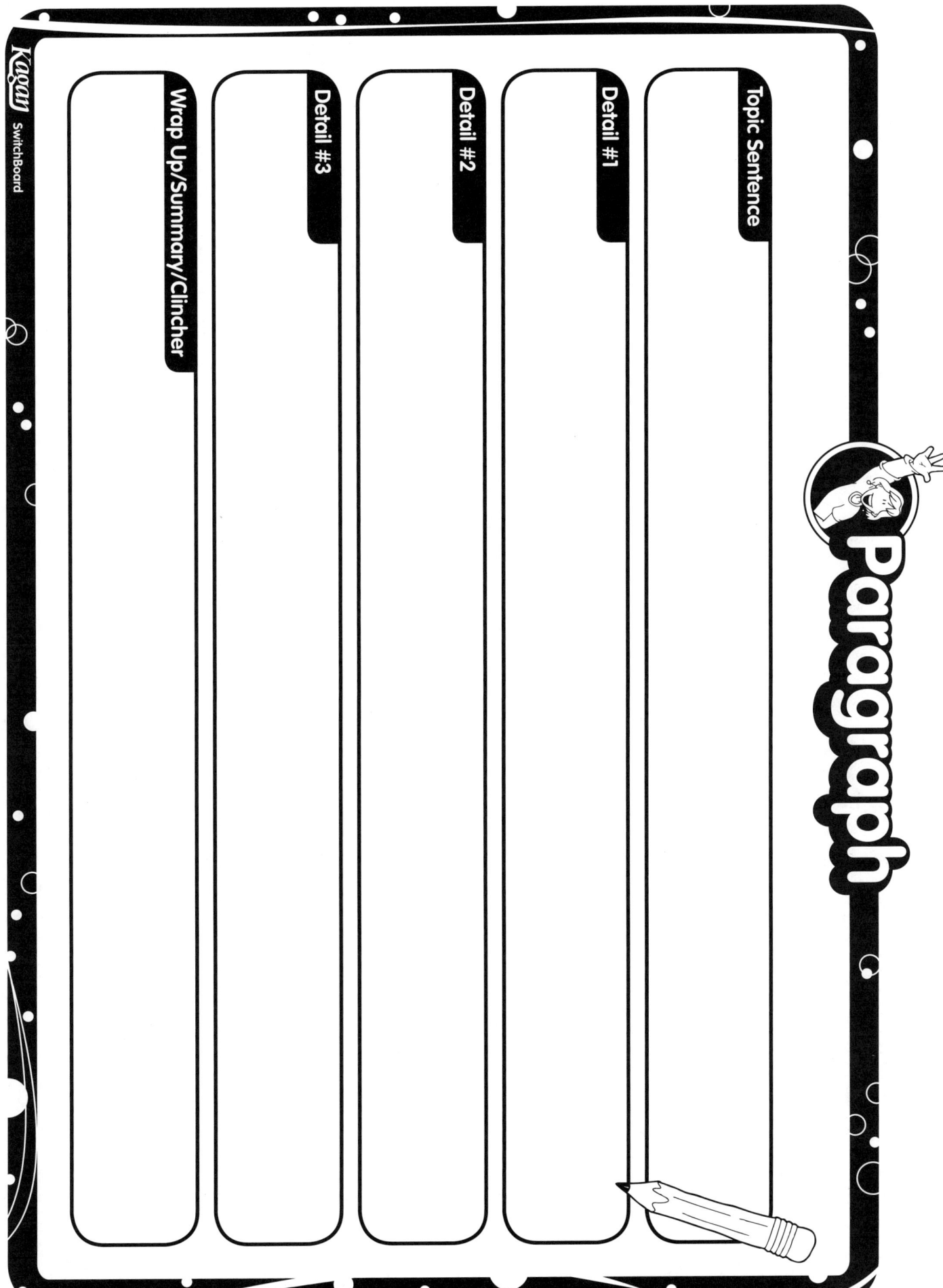

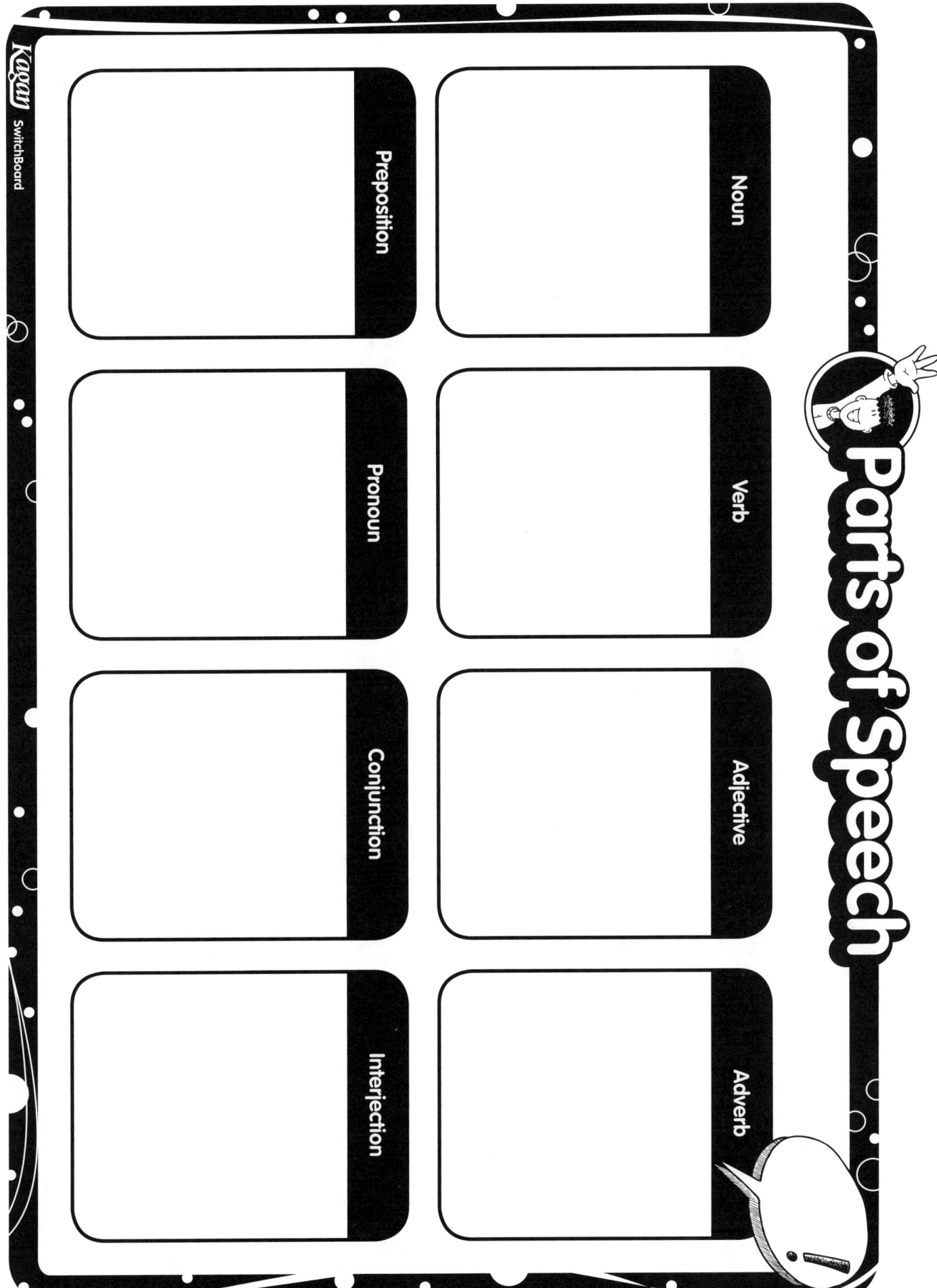

Aa Bb Cc Dd Ee Ff
Gg Hh Ii Jj Kk Ll Mm
Nn Oo Pp Qq Rr Ss Tt
Uu Vv Ww Xx Yy Zz

Printing

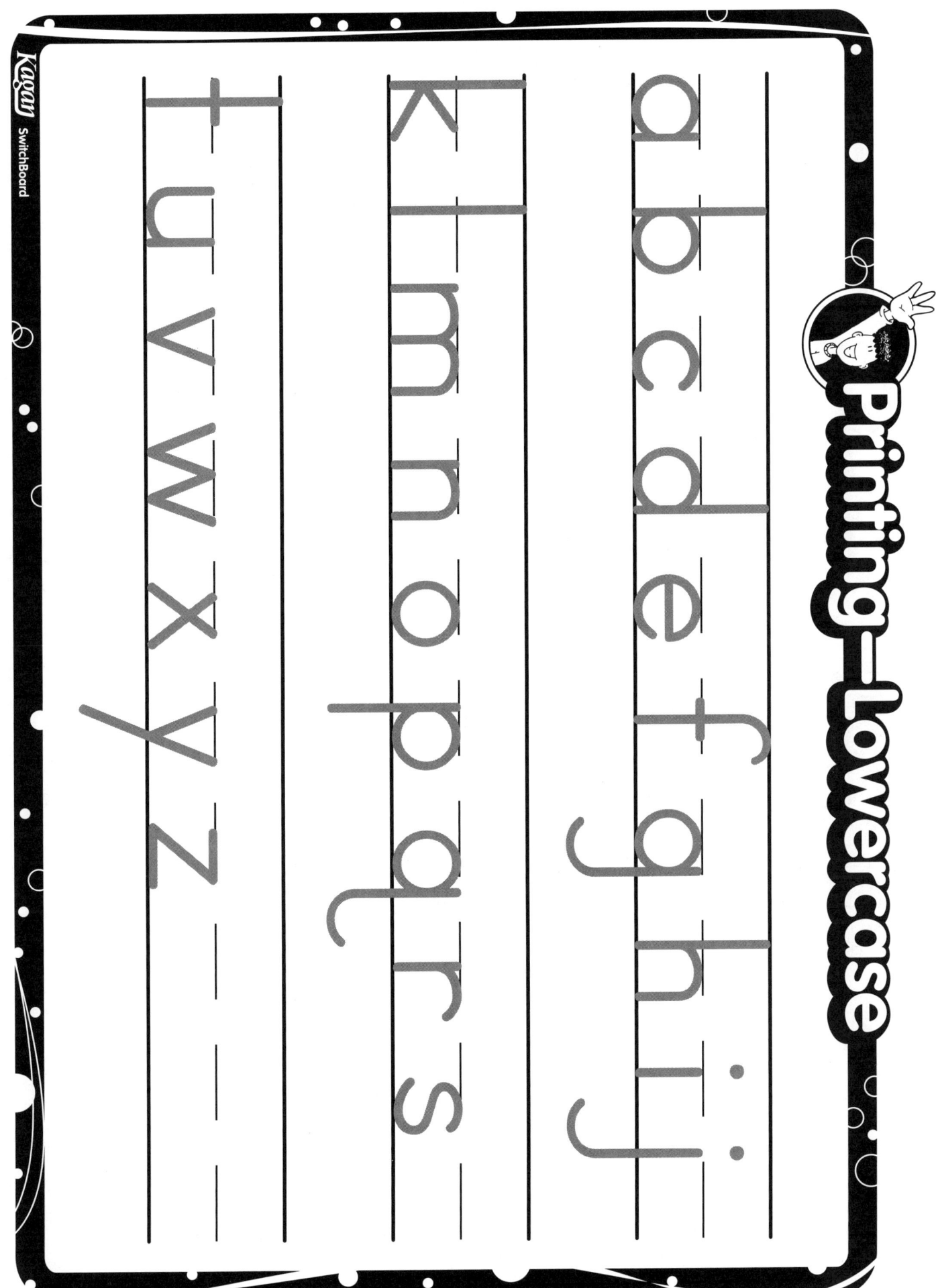

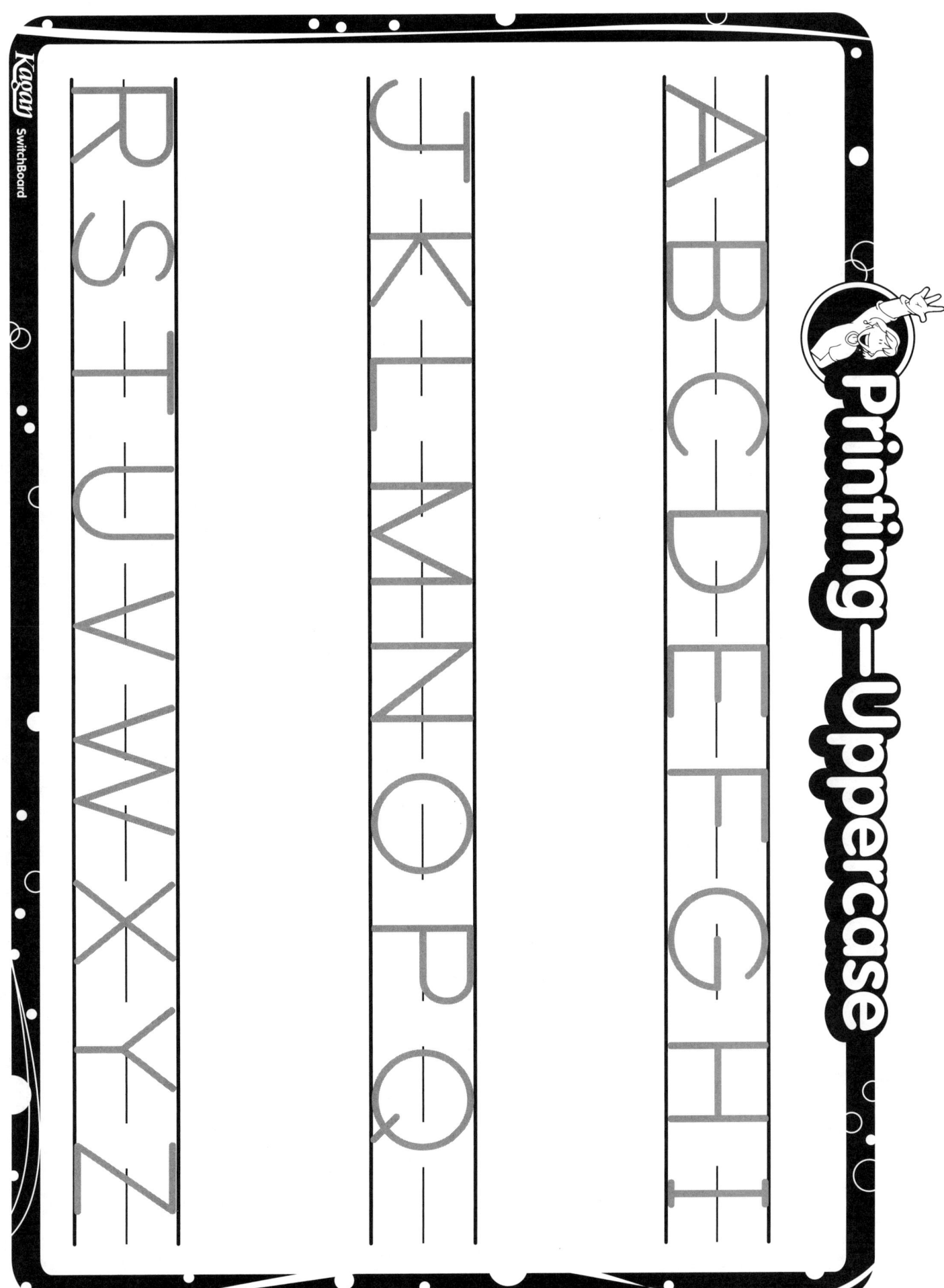

Story _____

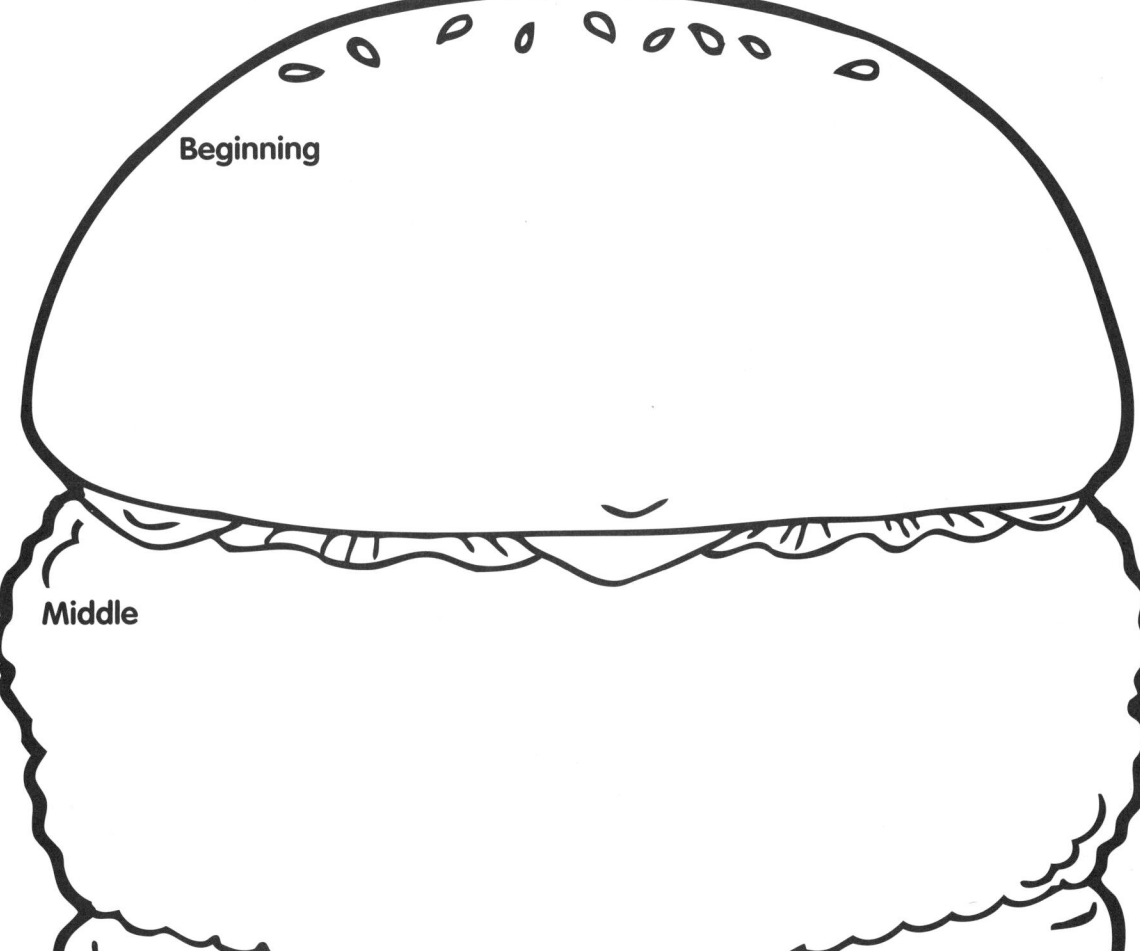

Beginning

Middle

End

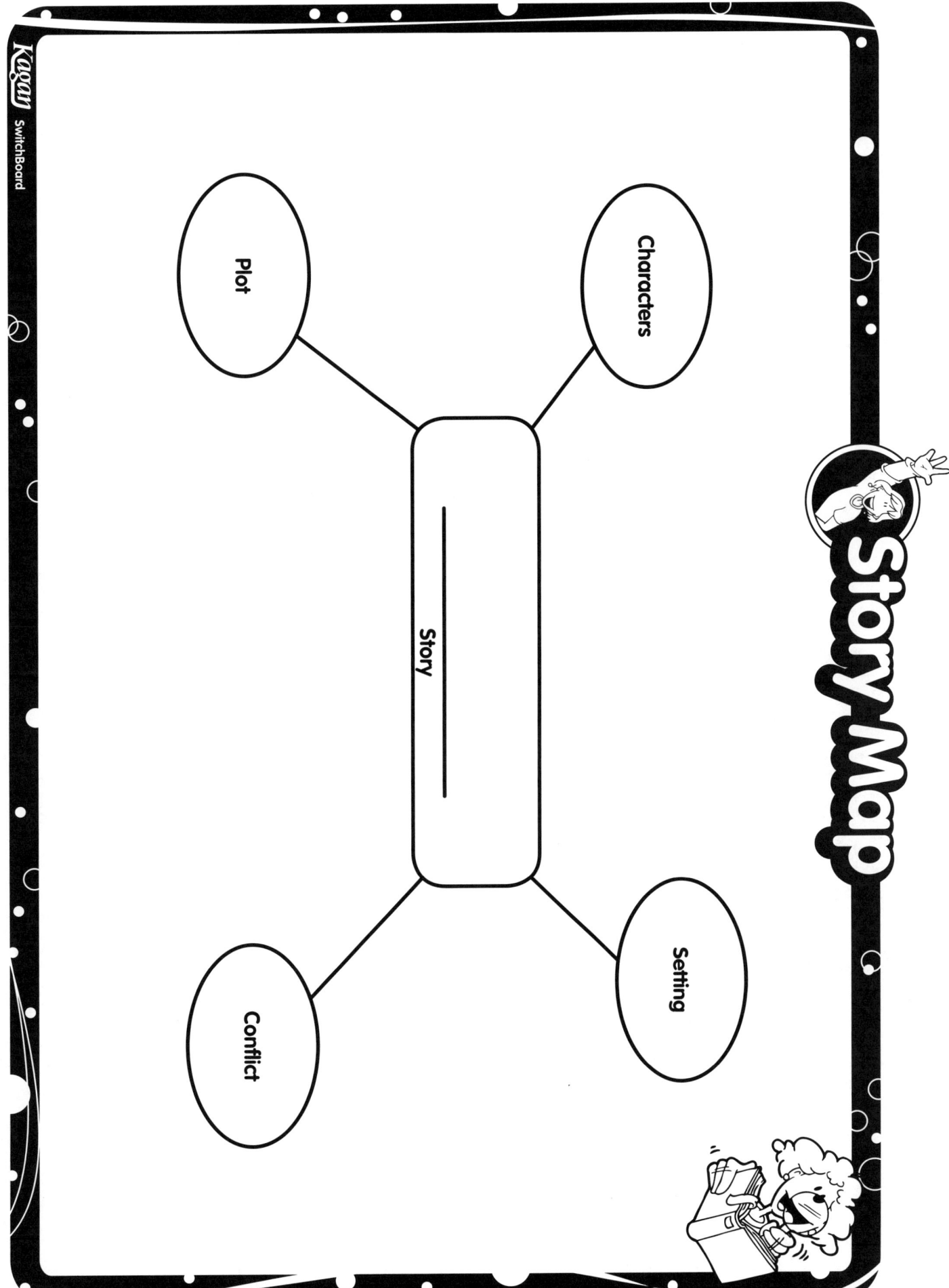

Story Plot Map

Story _____

Event

then…

Event

then…

Event

then…

Event

then…

Event

then…

Event

Vocabulary Term

Term

Drawing

Definition/Example

Vocabulary Terms

Word	Word
Drawing	Drawing

Word	Word
Drawing	Drawing

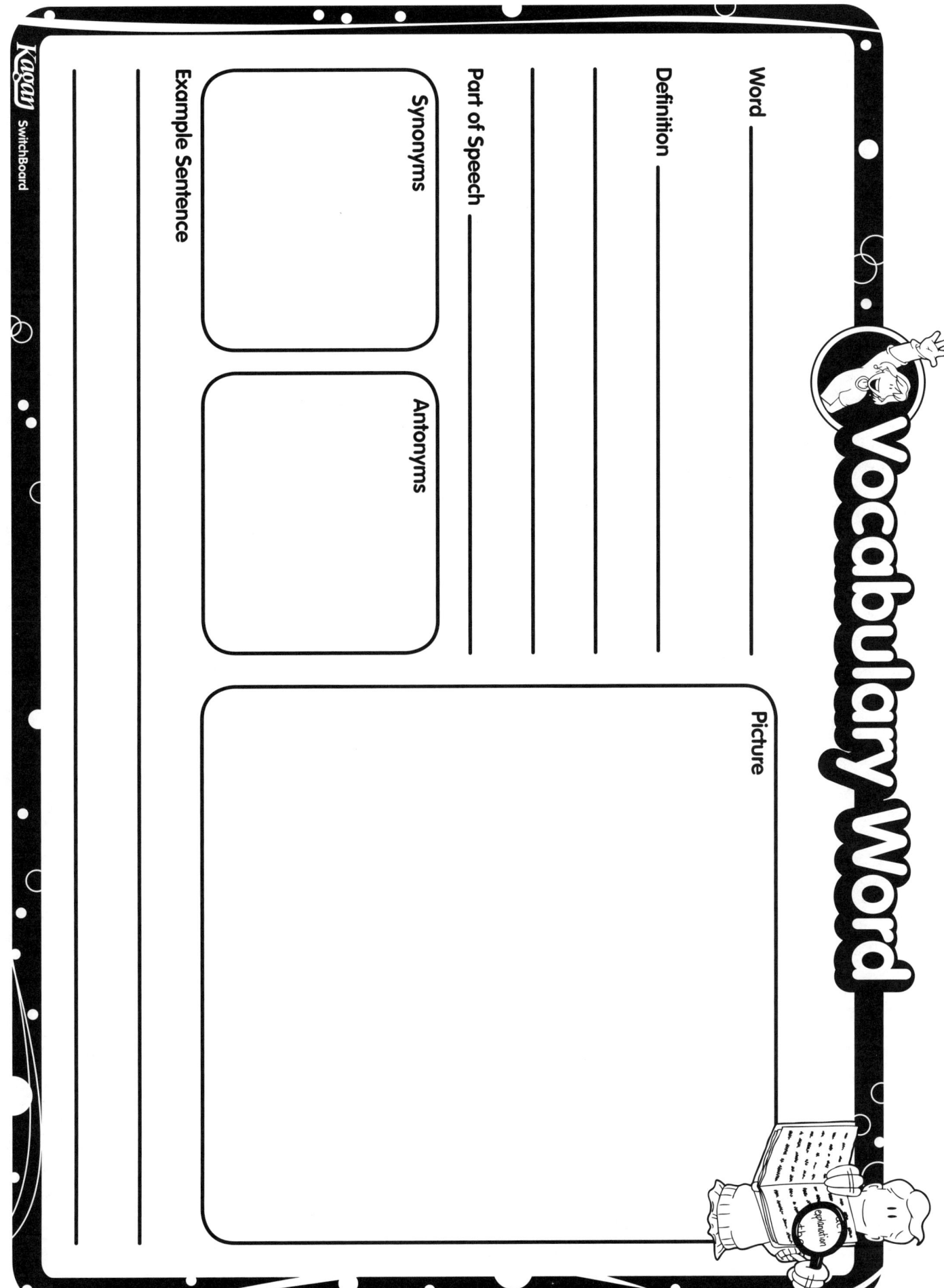

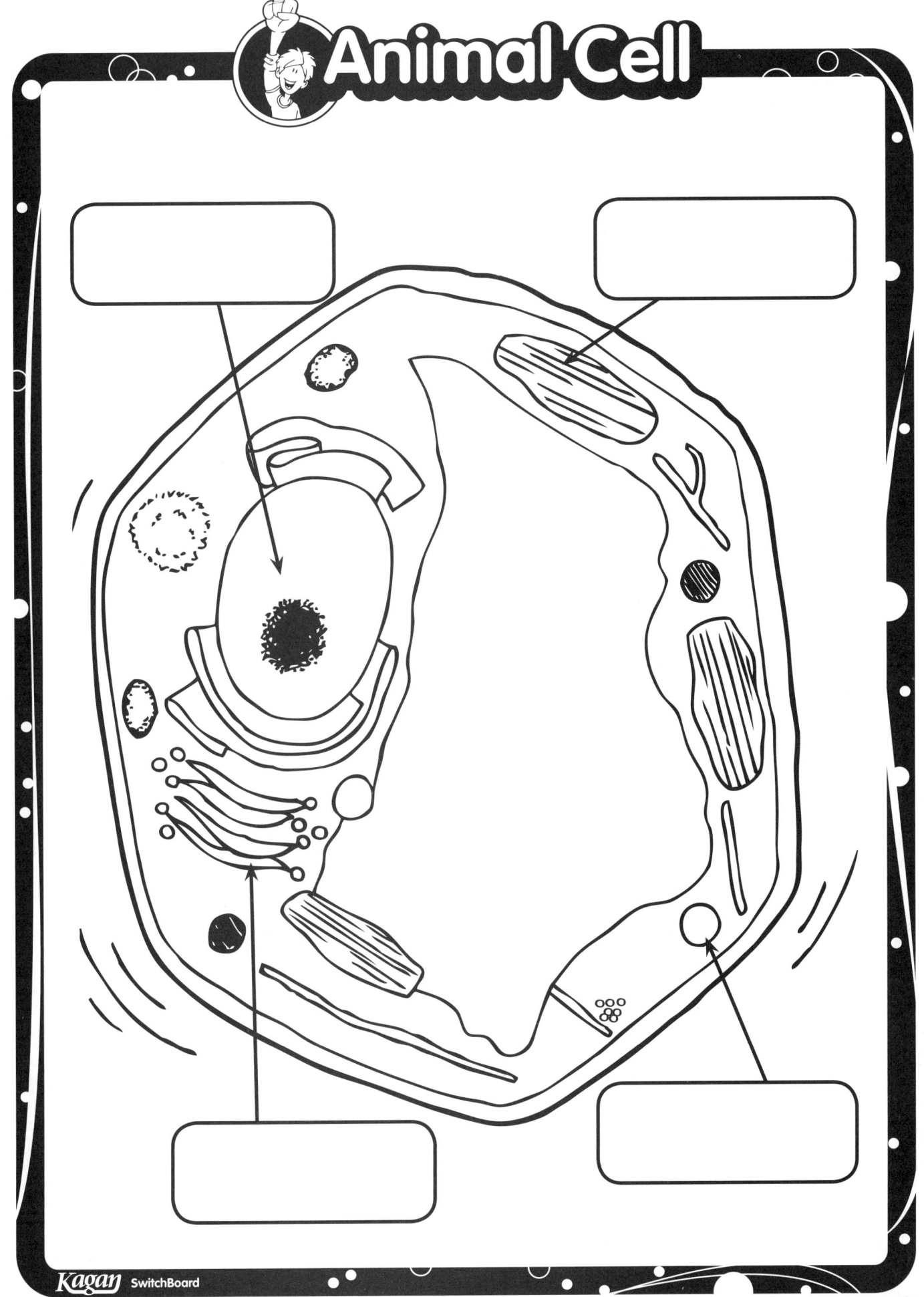

Animal Traits

Animal Name _____

Height _____

Weight _____

Size _____

Appearance _____

_____

_____

Diet	Habitat

Behavior	

Reproduction	Lifespan

Predators/Threats

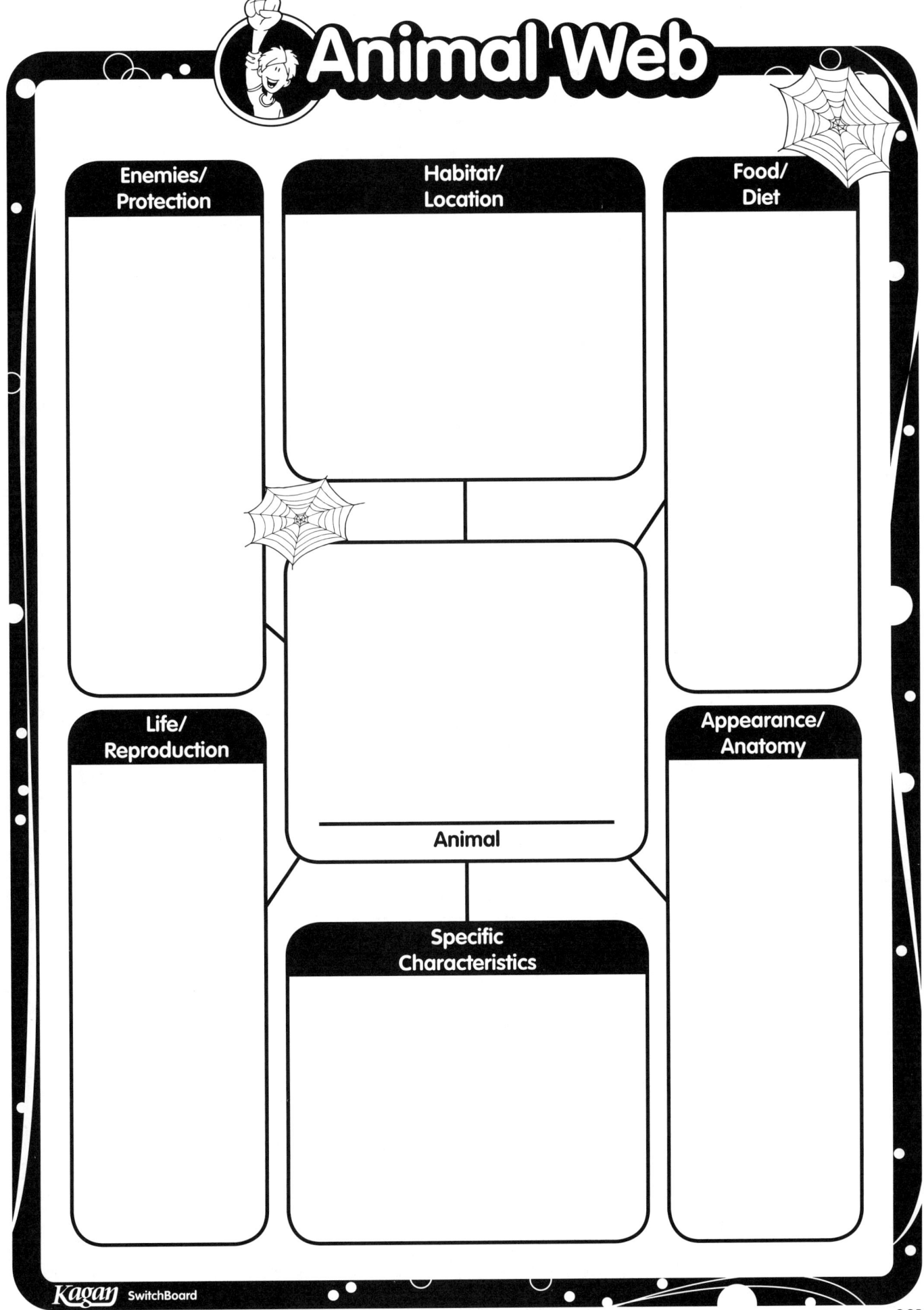

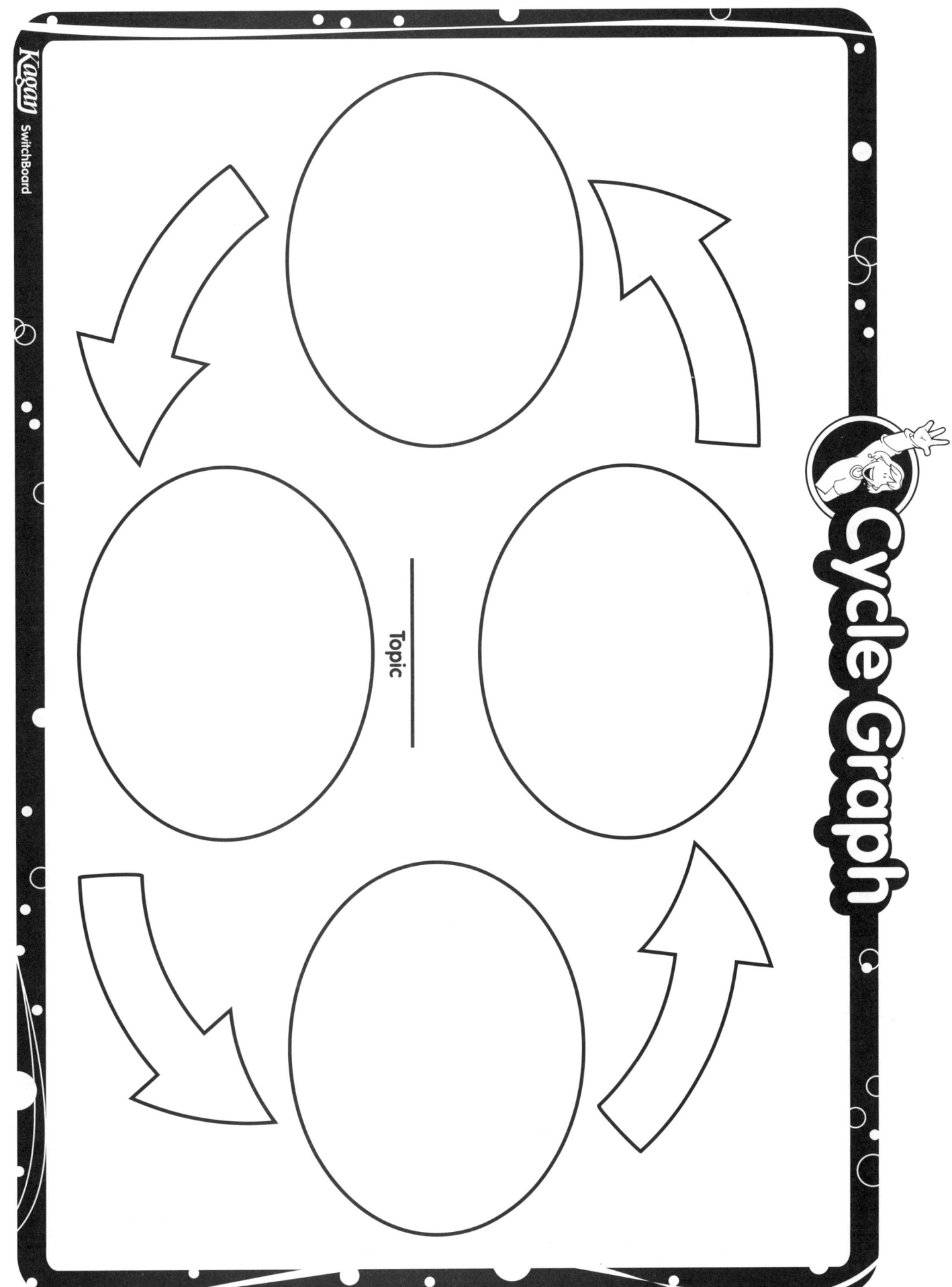

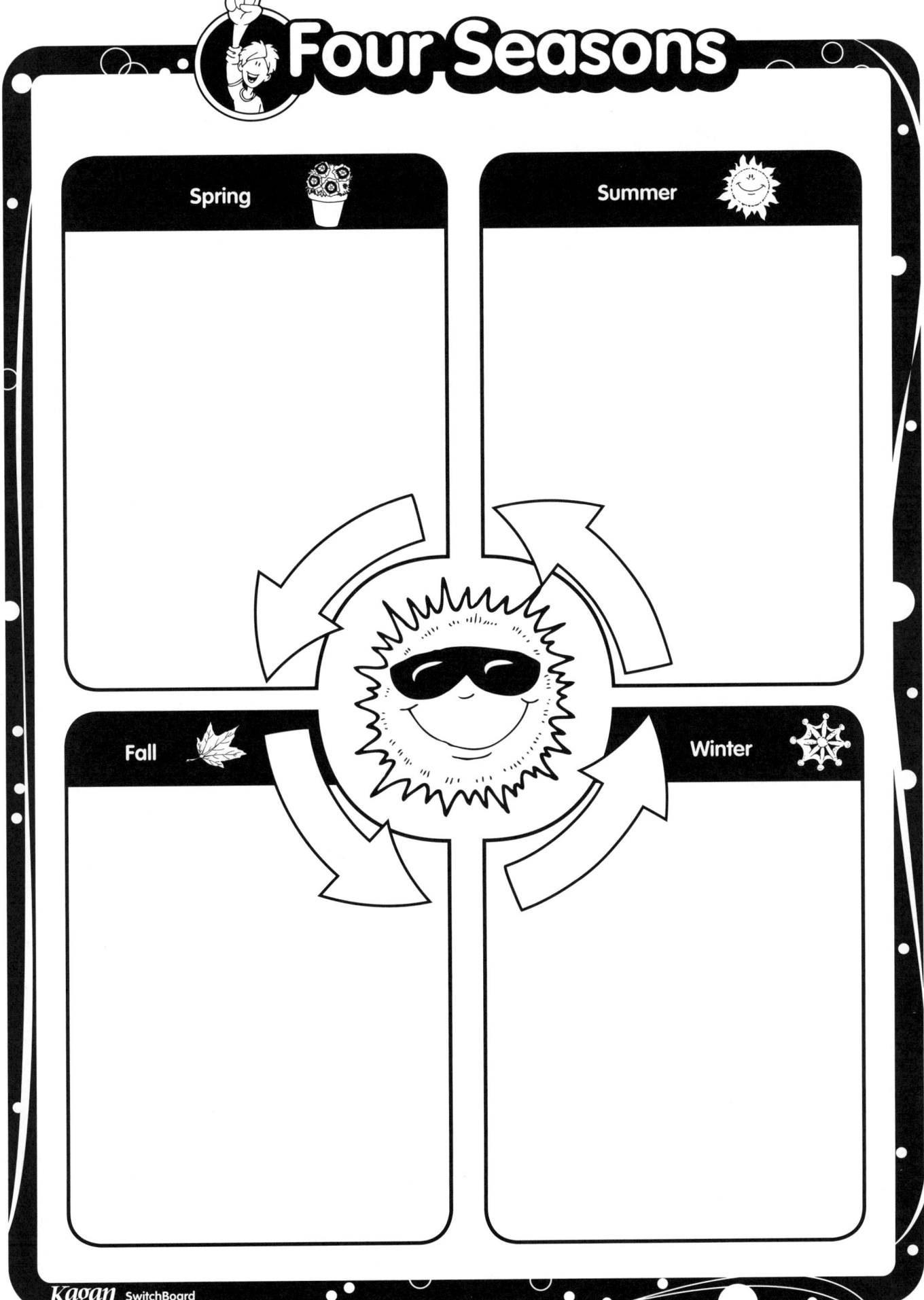

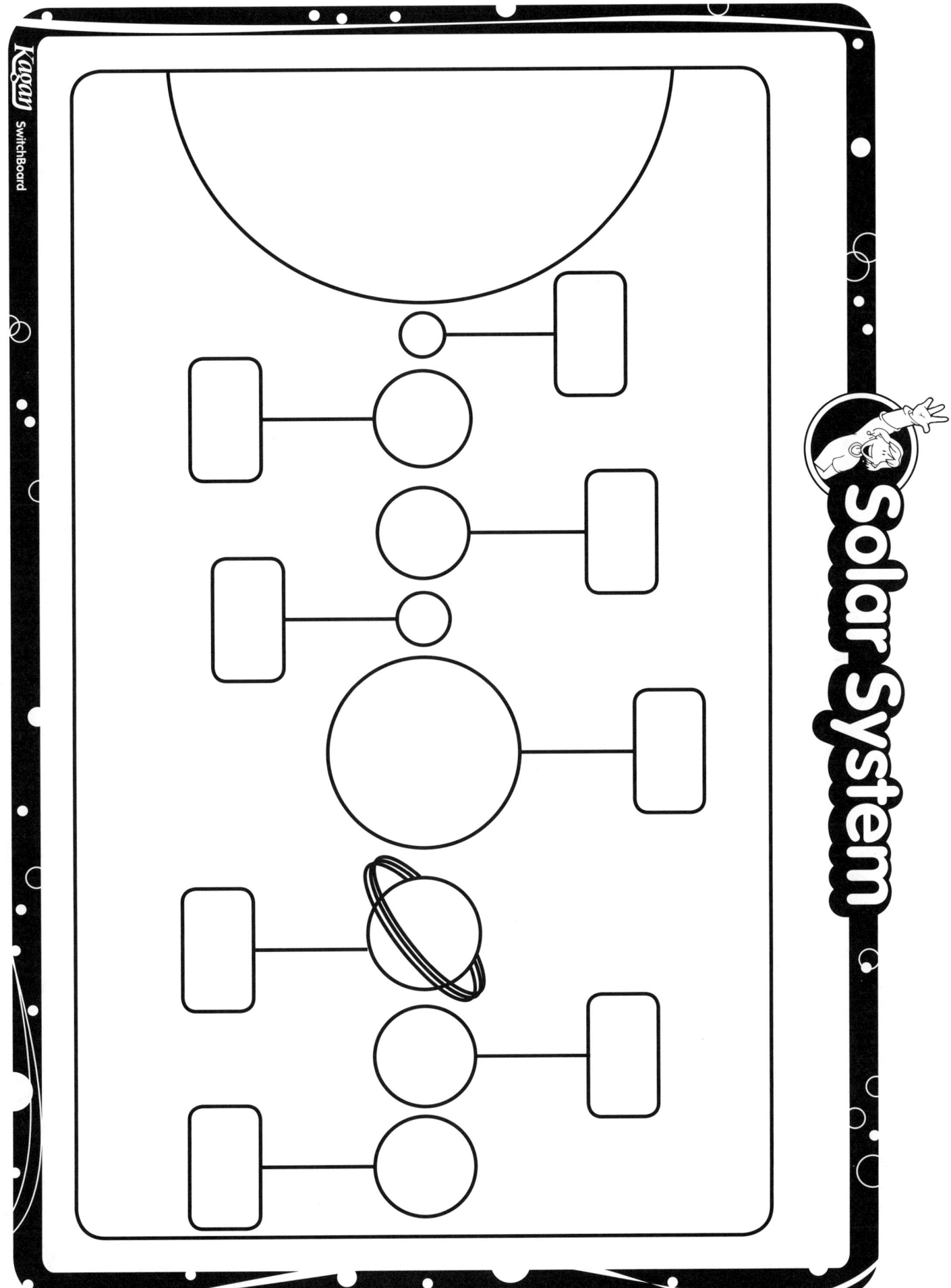

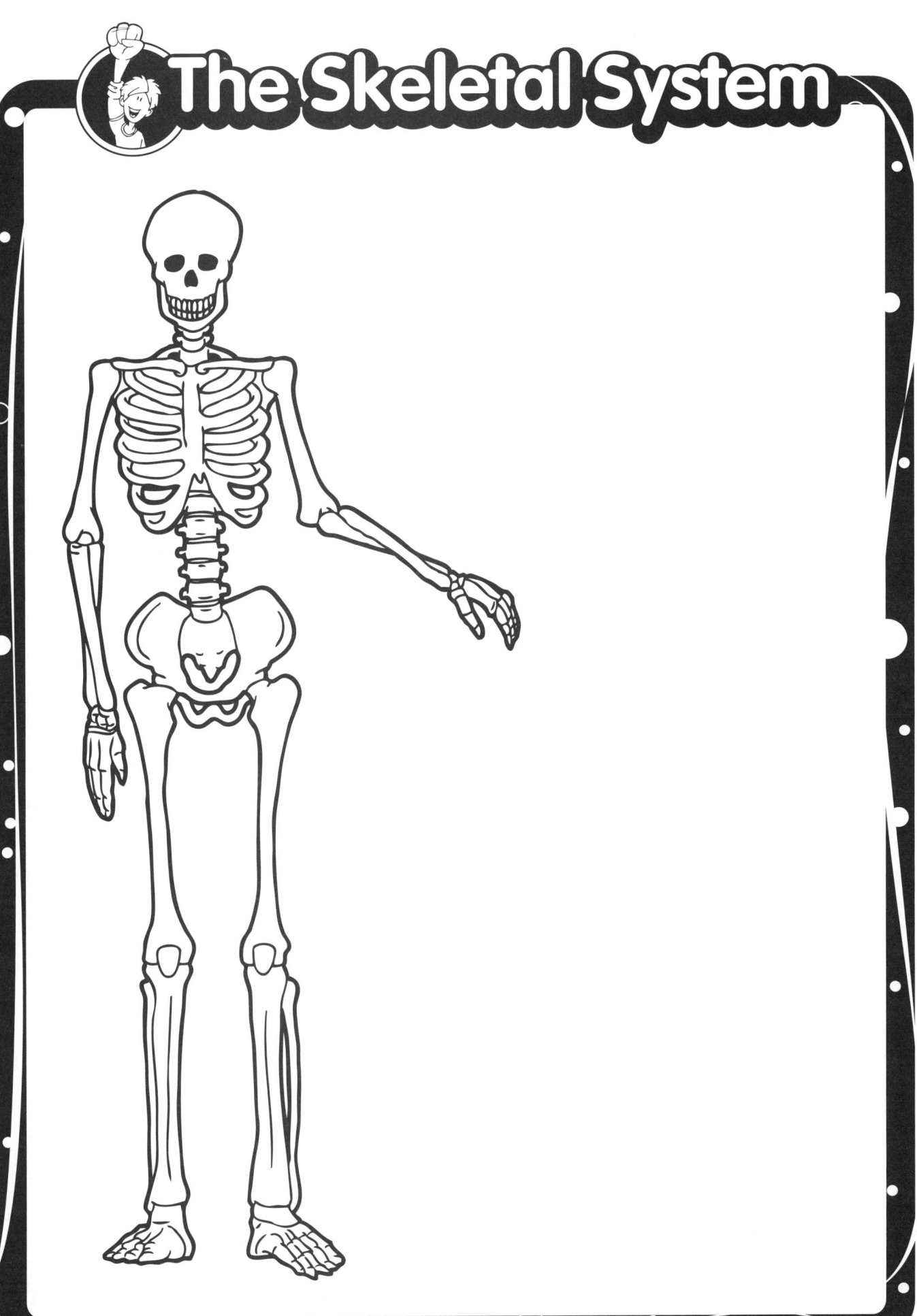

Volcano

Water Cycle

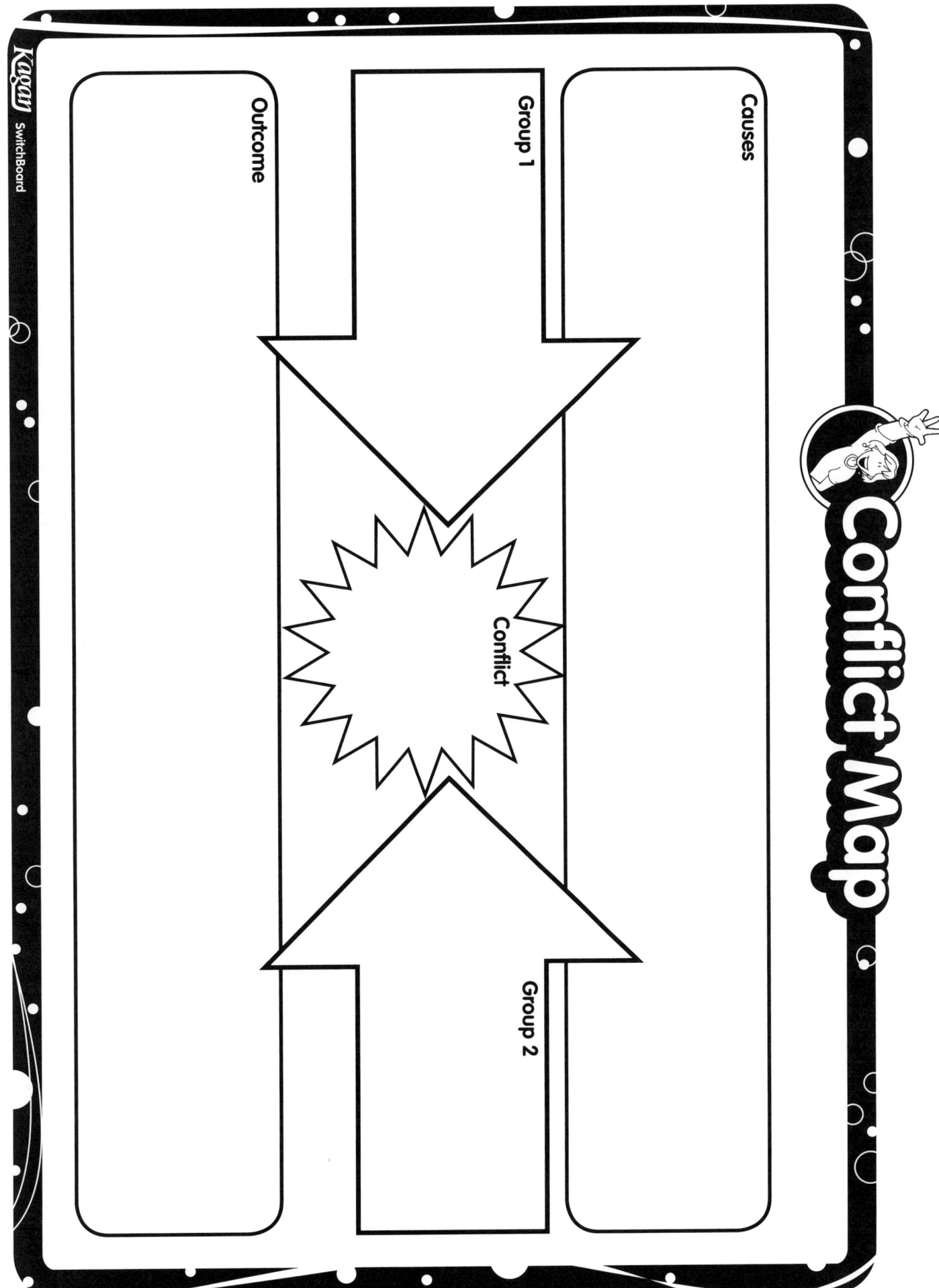

Country Facts

Country Name _____

Geography

Continent _____

Climate _____

Flag

People

Population _____

Religions _____

Languages _____

Government

Economy

Current Event

Article Title _____

Source _____

Who?

What?

Why?

Where?

When?

My Thoughts About the Event

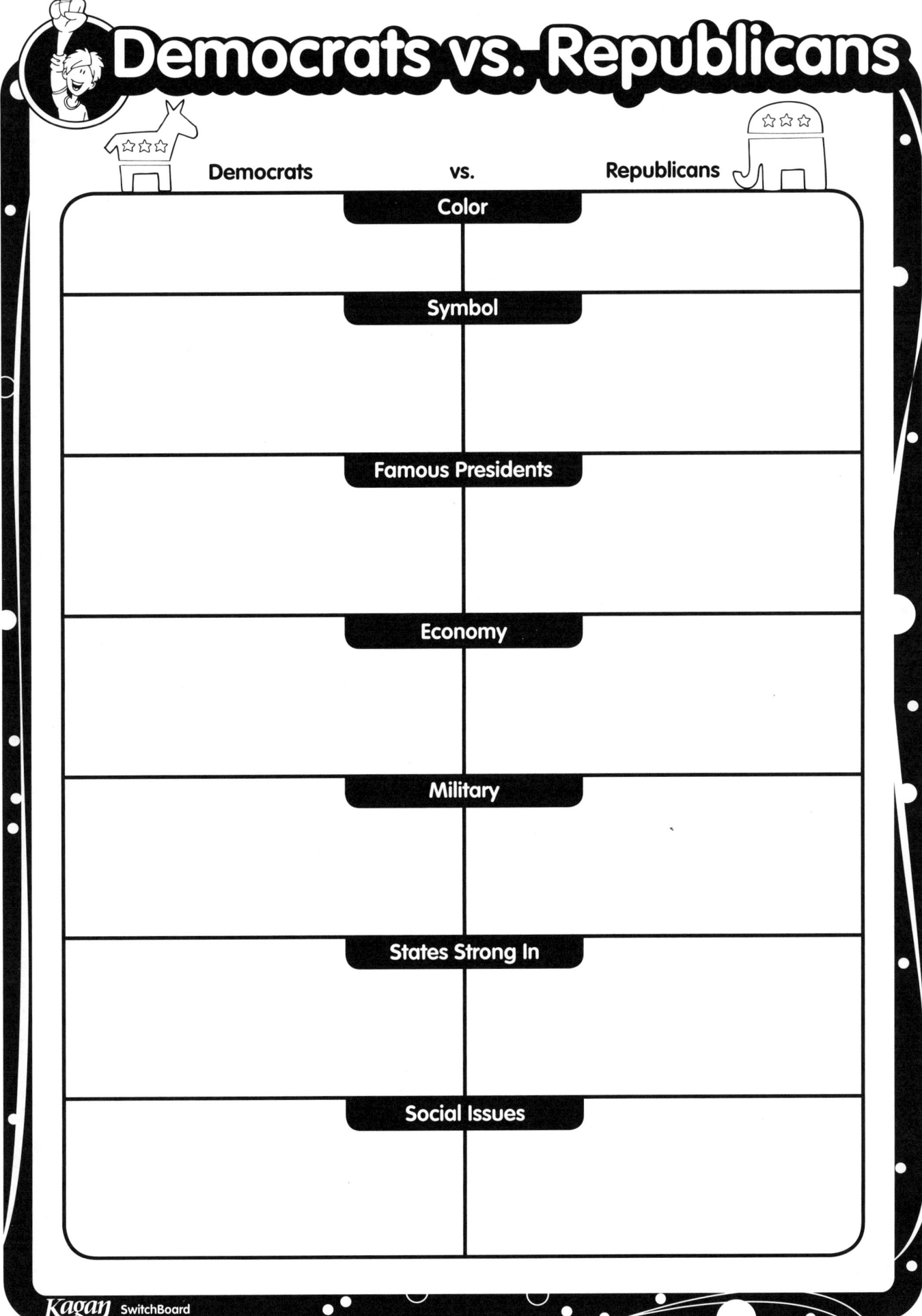

Event Timeline

Event _____

Date

Date

Date

Date

Date

Date

Famous Explorer

Name _____

Exploration Dates _____

Country _____

Searching for

Major Accomplishments

Gratefulness Journal

Three Things I'm Grateful For…

1.

2.

3.

Holiday

Holiday Name _____

Date(s) _____

Draw it

Reason for Holiday

How it is Celebrated

Map of Africa

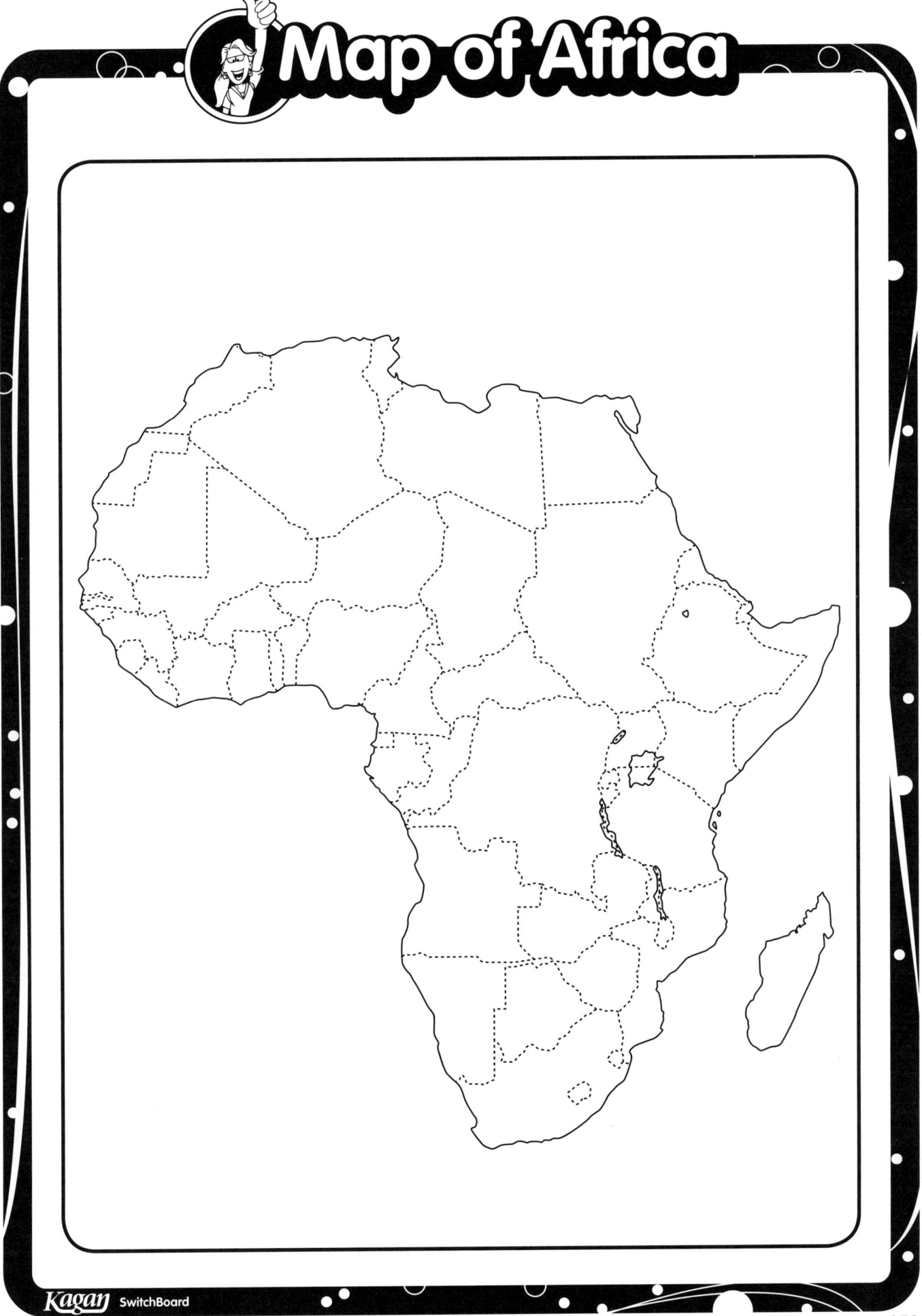

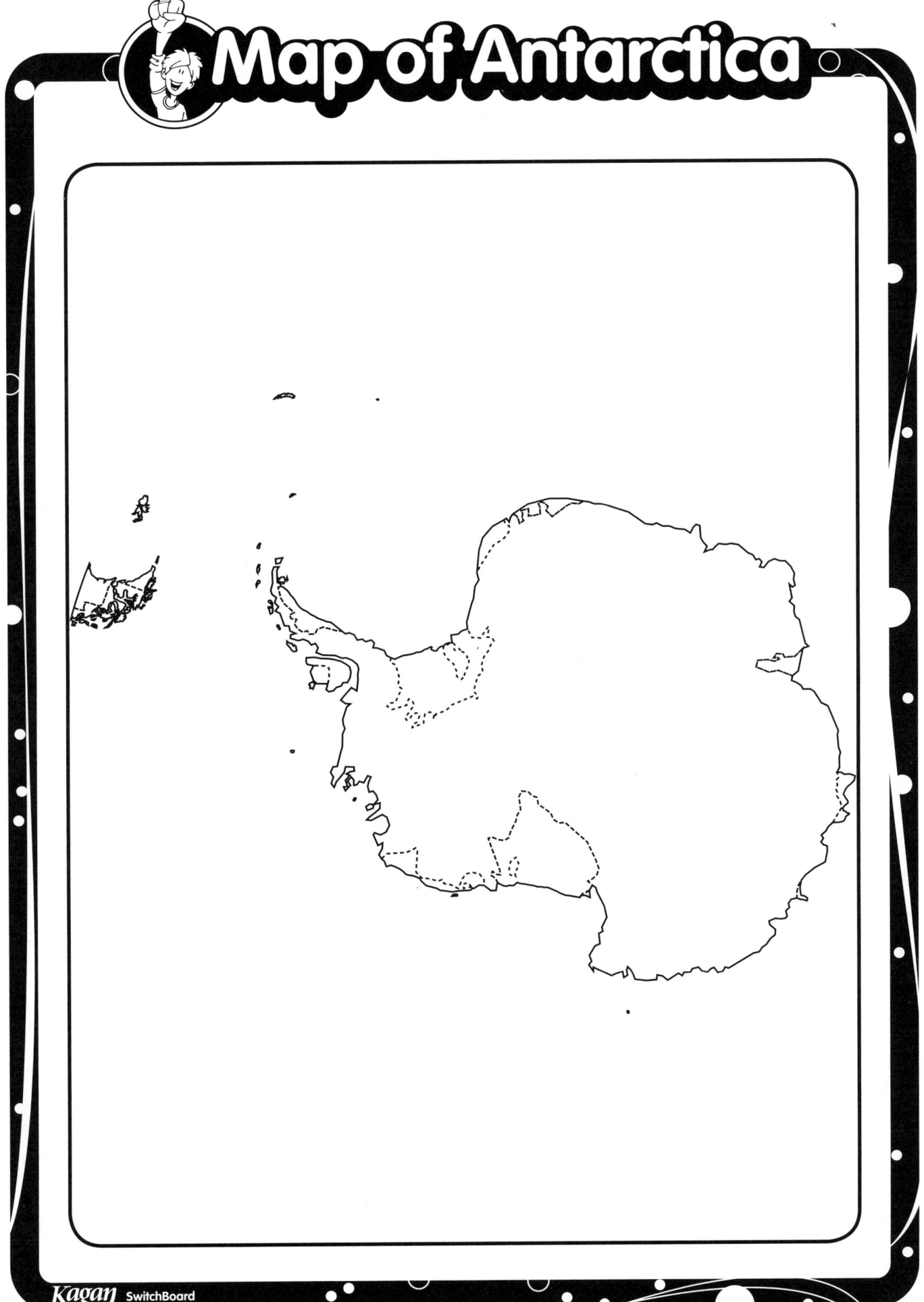

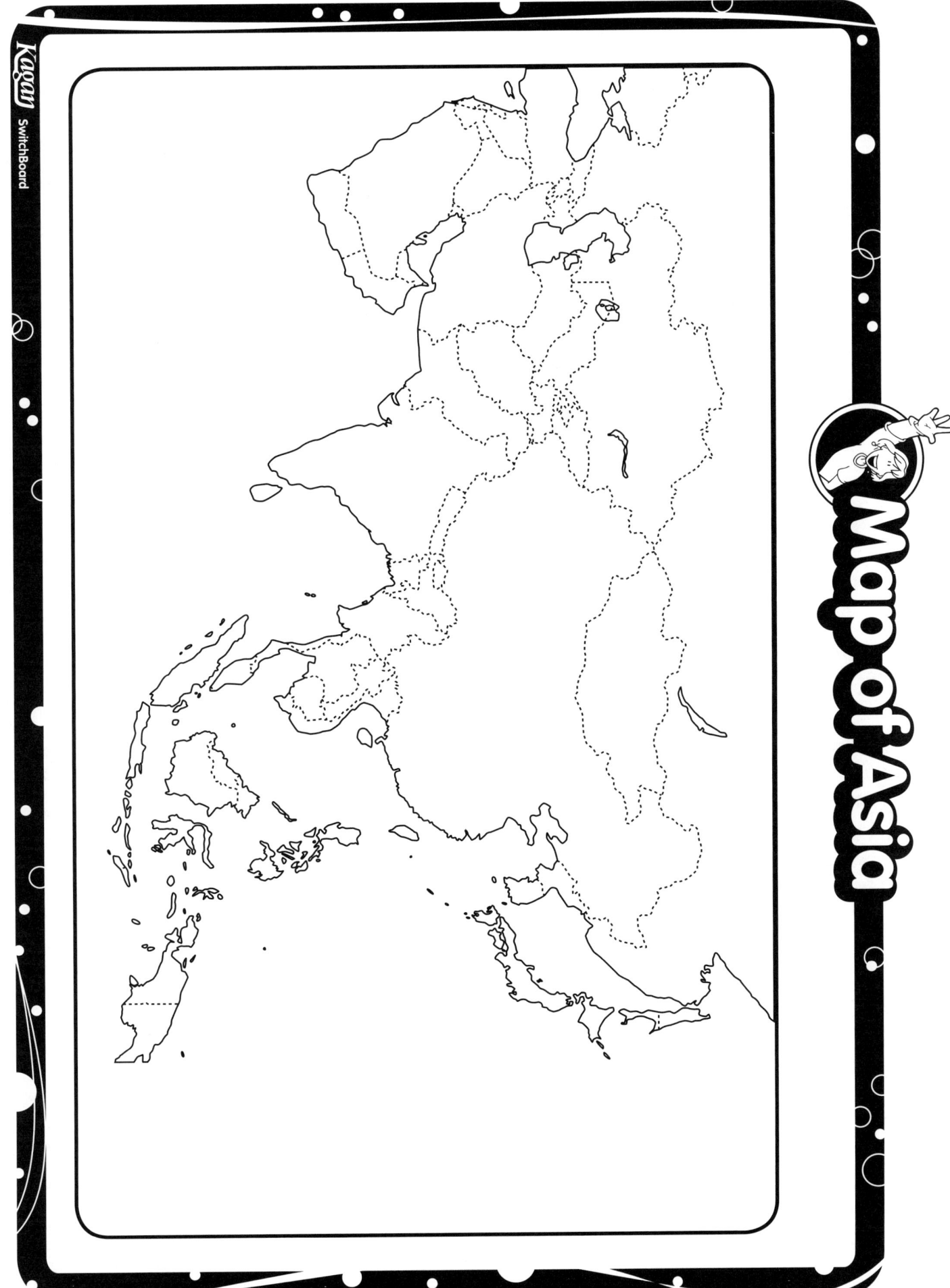

Map of Europe

Map of North America

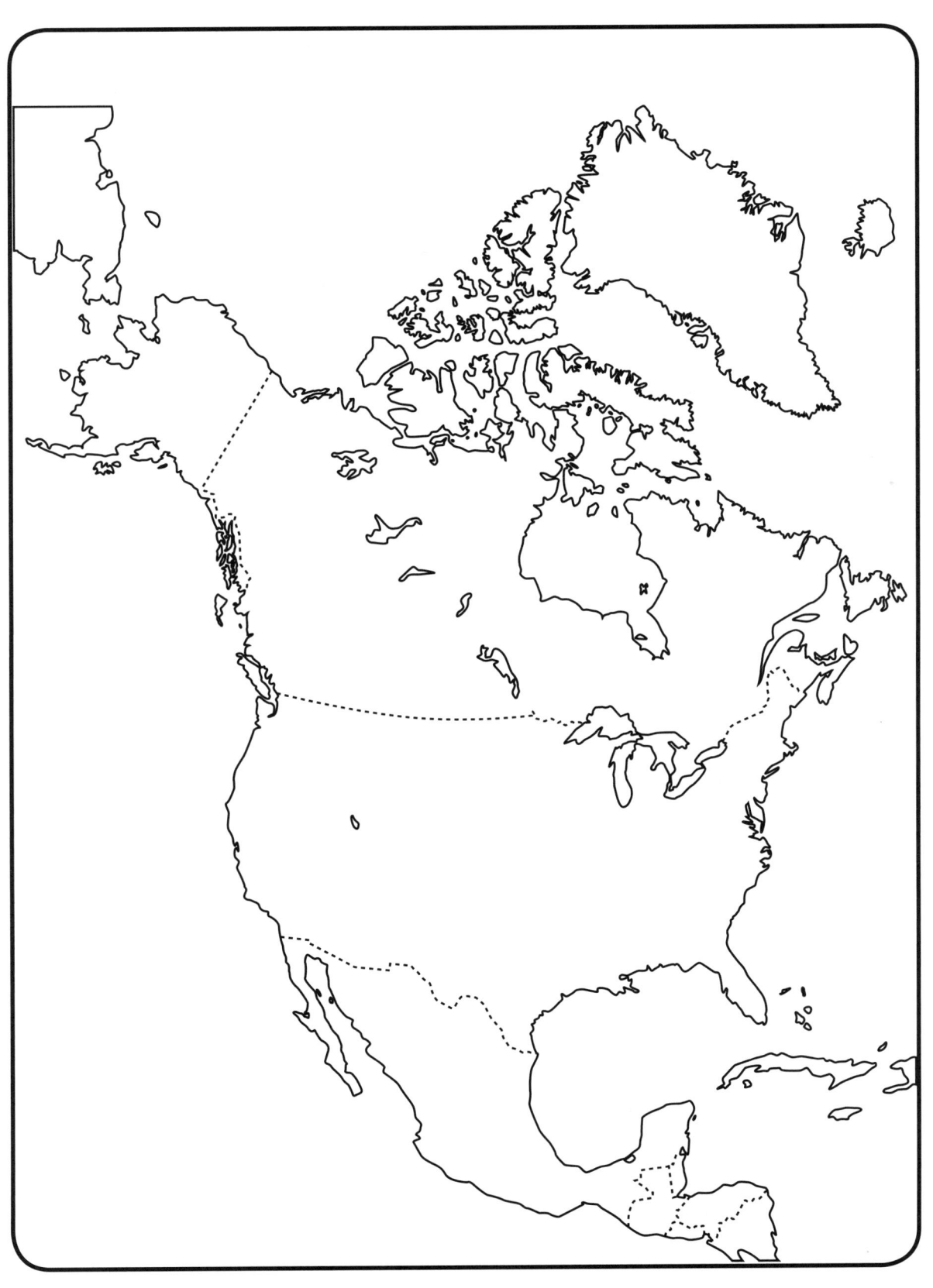

Map of South America

State Facts

State Name _____

Location _____

Capital _____

Flag

Motto _____

Symbols

Flower _____

Tree _____

Bird _____

Fish _____

Nickname _____

Largest Cities _____

Interesting Notes _____

_____

_____

Three Branches of Government

Legislature

Executive

Judicial

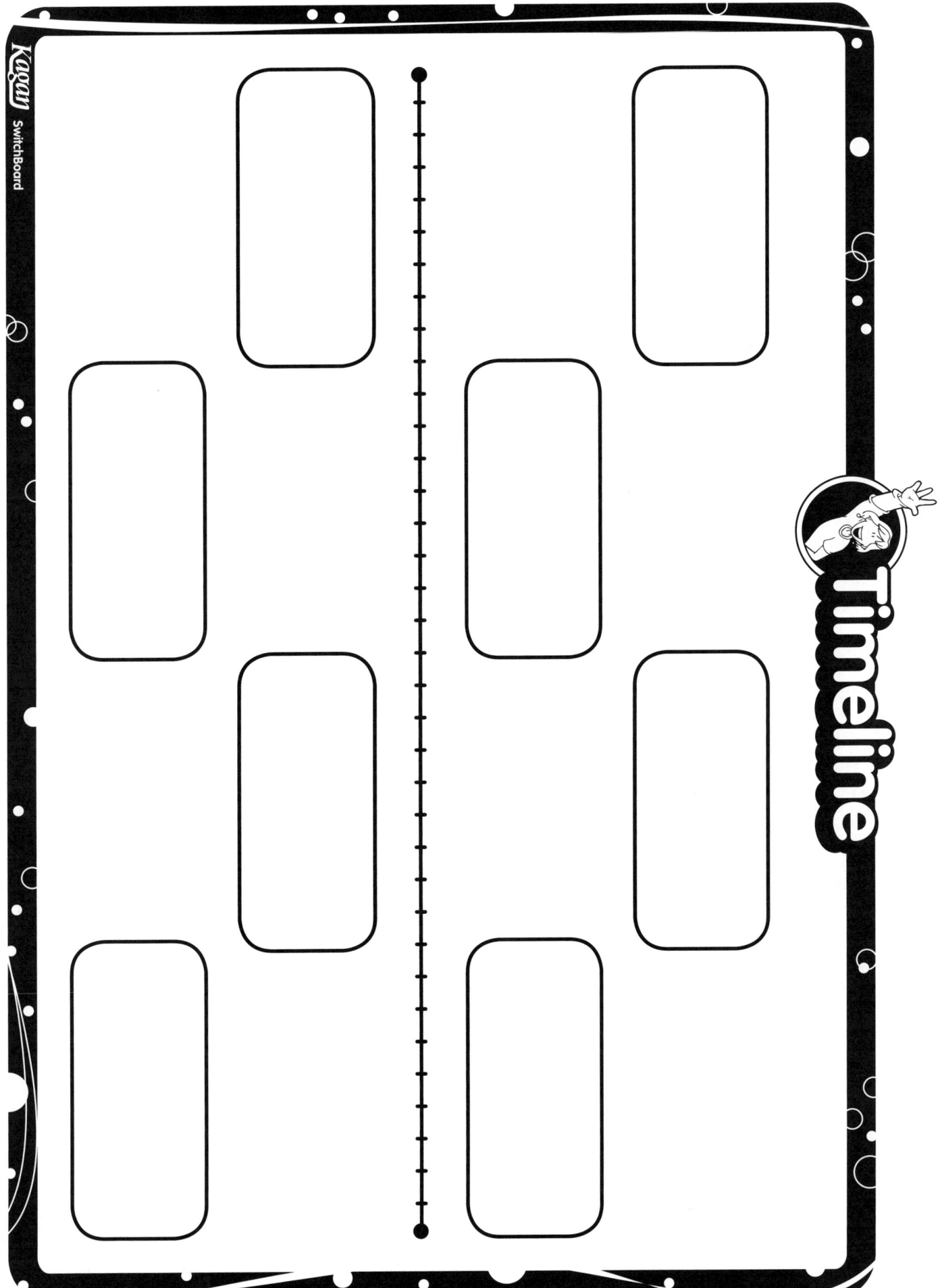

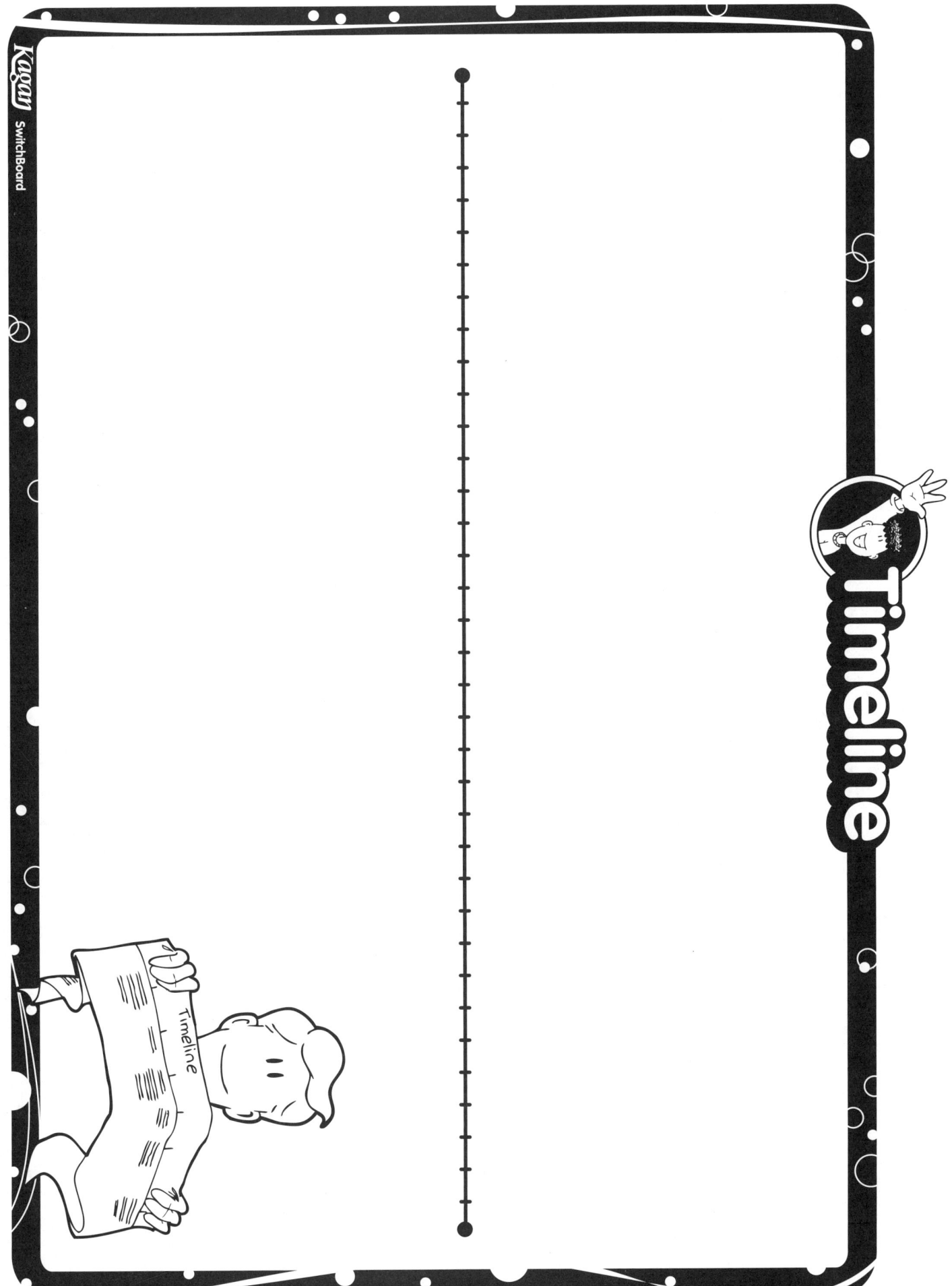

U.S. President

President _____

★ **Term** _____

★ **President Number** _____

★ **Political Party** _____

★ **Prior Occupation** _____

_____

★ **Accomplishments as President** ★

_____
_____
_____
_____
_____
_____
_____
_____
_____

War

Name of War _____

Dates _____

Between [ ] & [ ]

Causes

Outcome

World Leader

Name _____

Country _____

Dates _____

Major Accomplishments | **Illustration**

Accomplishment #1

Accomplishment #2

Accomplishment #3

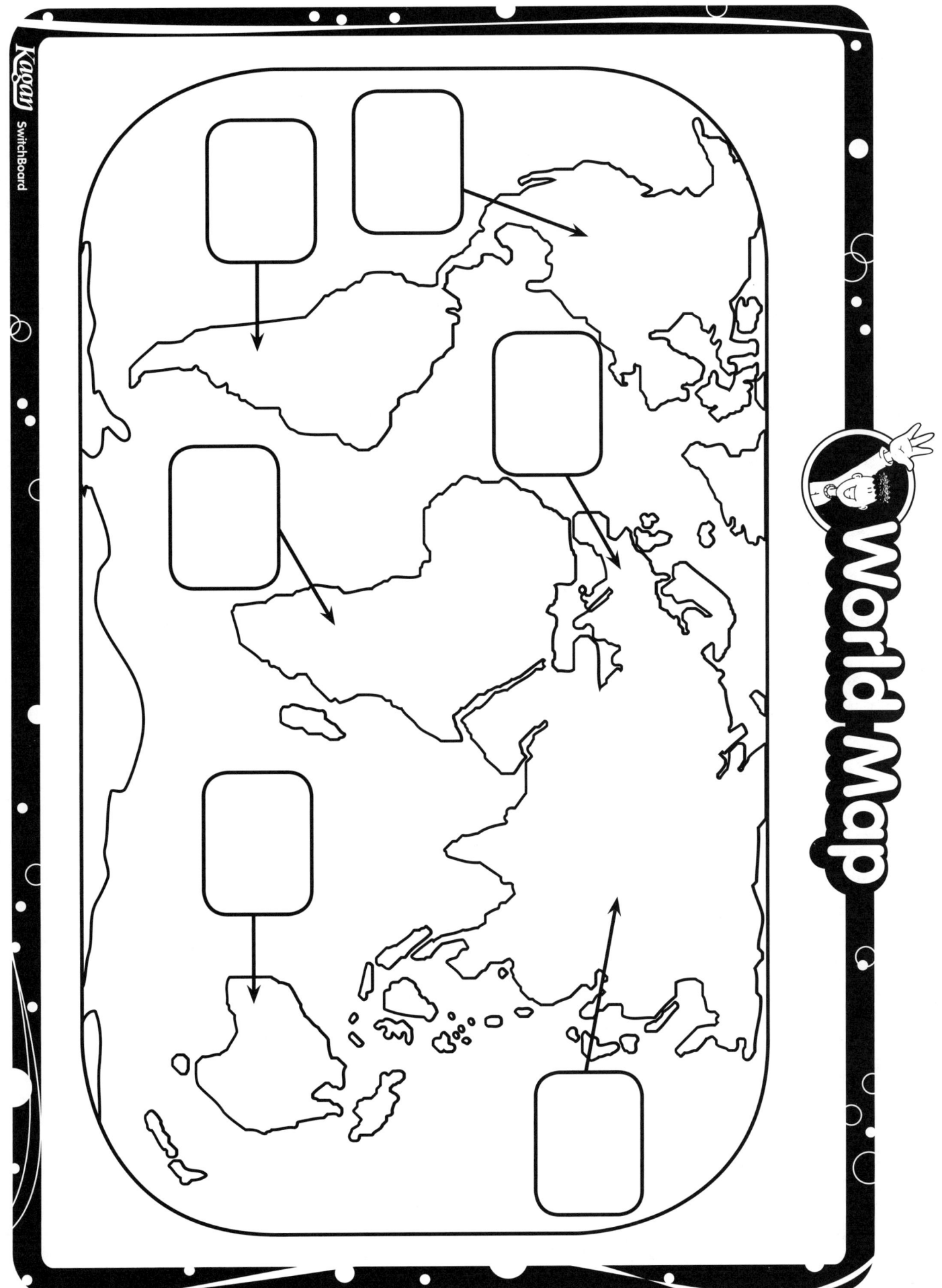

World Religion

Religion Name _____

Leaders

Major Regions

Beliefs

Holidays & Traditions

History

Symbols

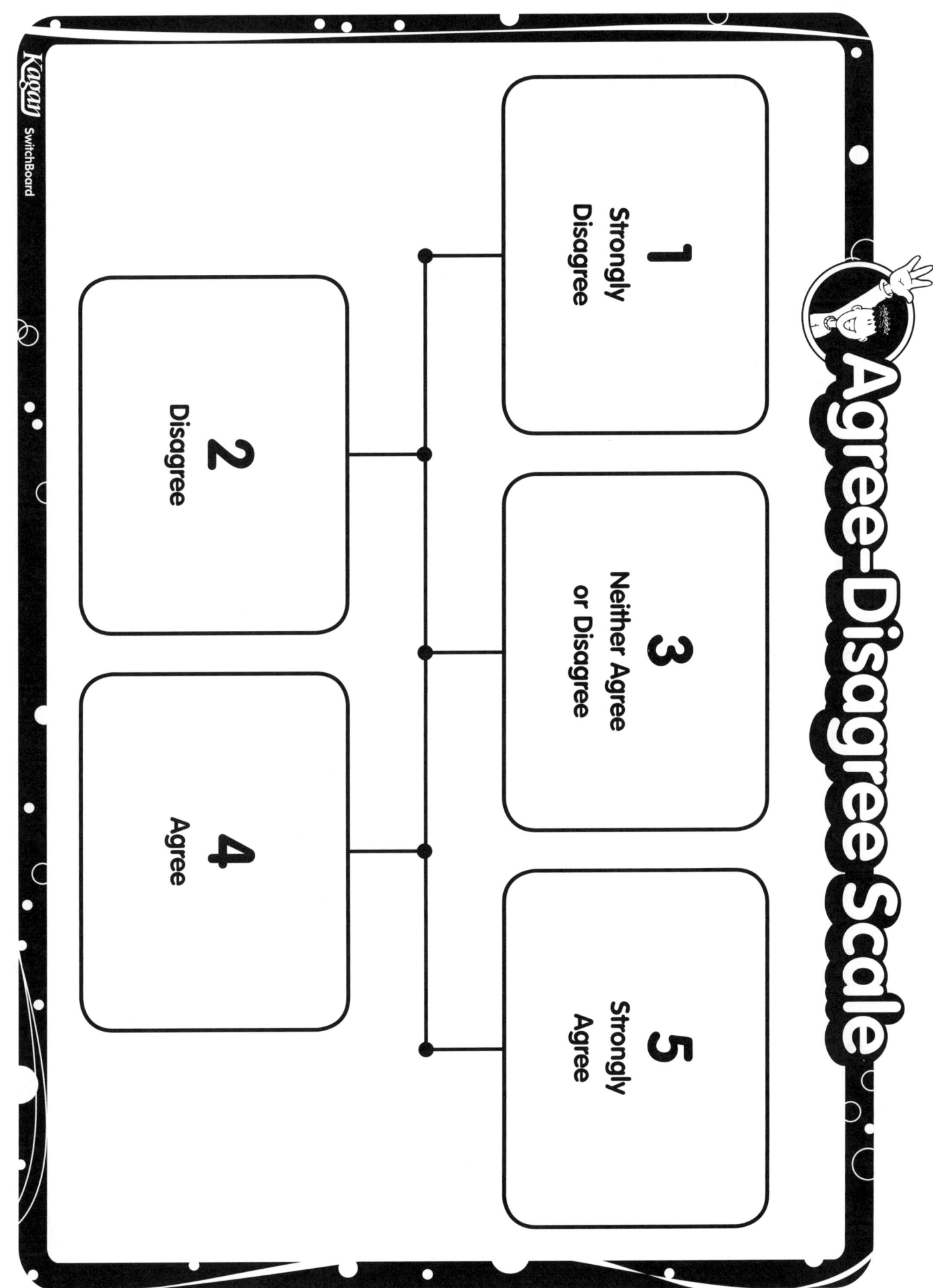

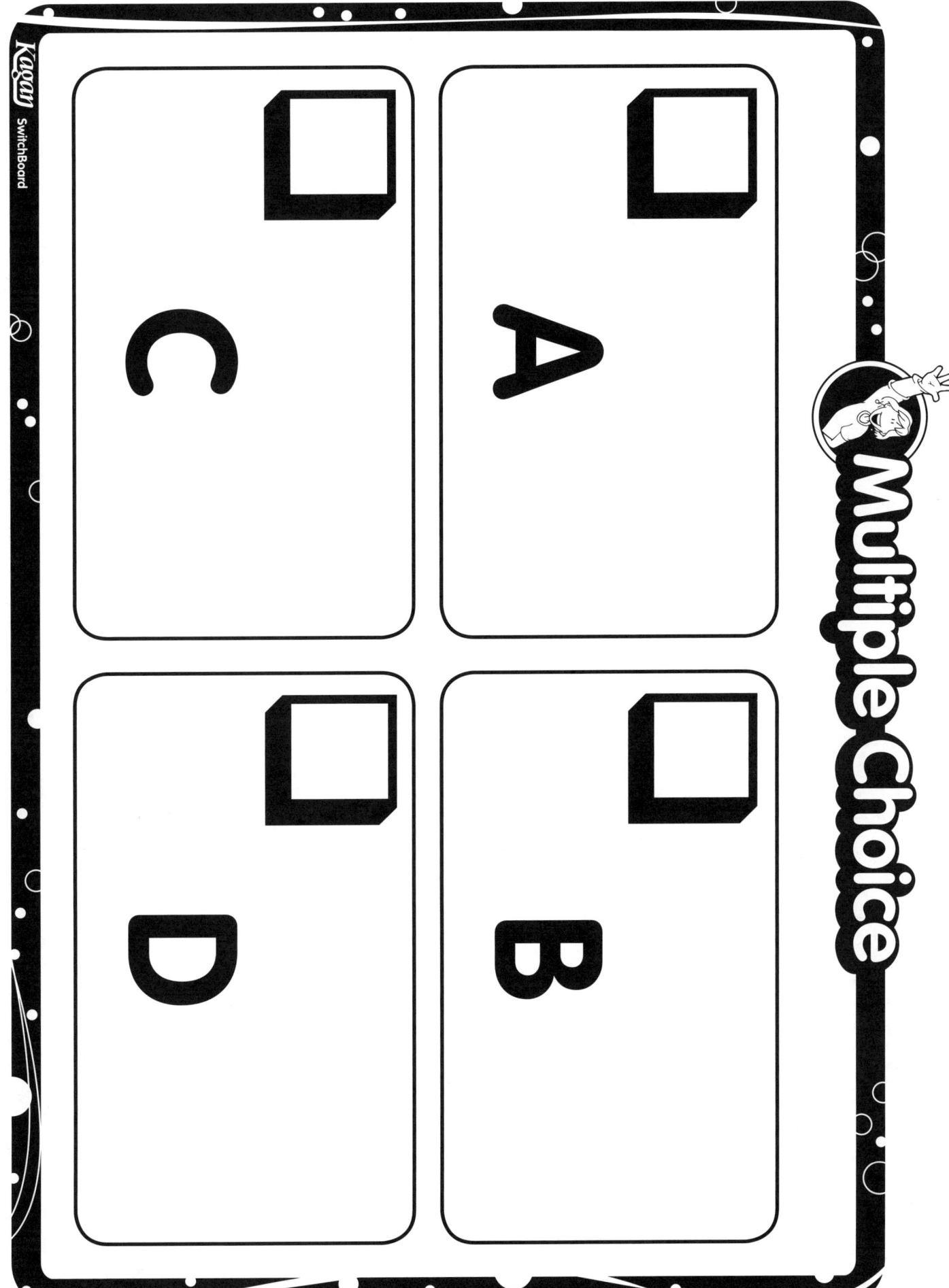

Battleship

Sink your opponent's ships by guessing the coordinates. Mark misses with an O. Mark hits with an X.

	1	2	3	4	5	6	7	8	9	10
A										
B										
C										
D										
E										
F										
G										
H										
I										
J										

Ships
Draw your ships on your grid.

1 Carrier = 5 squares

2 Battleships = 4 squares each

3 Destroyers = 2 squares each

2 Cruisers = 3 squares each

1 Submarine = 3 squares

Bulls and Cows—3-Digit

Write a secret code in the box below. Find a partner and take turns guessing each other's secret code. After your partner guesses, announce how many bulls and cows he or she received.
- Bull = Correct number in correct place.
- Cow = Correct number in wrong place.

Secret Code

My Guesses

	Bulls	Cows			Bulls	Cows
1	___	___		11	___	___
2	___	___		12	___	___
3	___	___		13	___	___
4	___	___		14	___	___
5	___	___		15	___	___
6	___	___		16	___	___
7	___	___		17	___	___
8	___	___		18	___	___
9	___	___		19	___	___
10	___	___		20	___	___

Bulls and Cows—4-Digit

Write a secret code in the box below. Find a partner and take turns guessing each other's secret code. After your partner guesses, announce how many bulls and cows he or she received.
- Bull = Correct number in correct place.
- Cow = Correct number in wrong place.

Secret Code

My Guesses

	Bulls	Cows			Bulls	Cows
1			11			
2			12			
3			13			
4			14			
5			15			
6			16			
7			17			
8			18			
9			19			
10			20			

Capture Boxes

Take turns drawing one line to connect the dots. The person who captures a box, writes his or her initials in the box and gets to go again. The person who captures the most boxes wins.

Capture Boxes

Take turns drawing one line to connect the dots. The person who captures a box, writes his or her initials in the box and gets to go again. The person who captures the most boxes wins.

Five in a Row

With a partner, take turns writing an X or O in each box. The person who gets five in a row first wins.

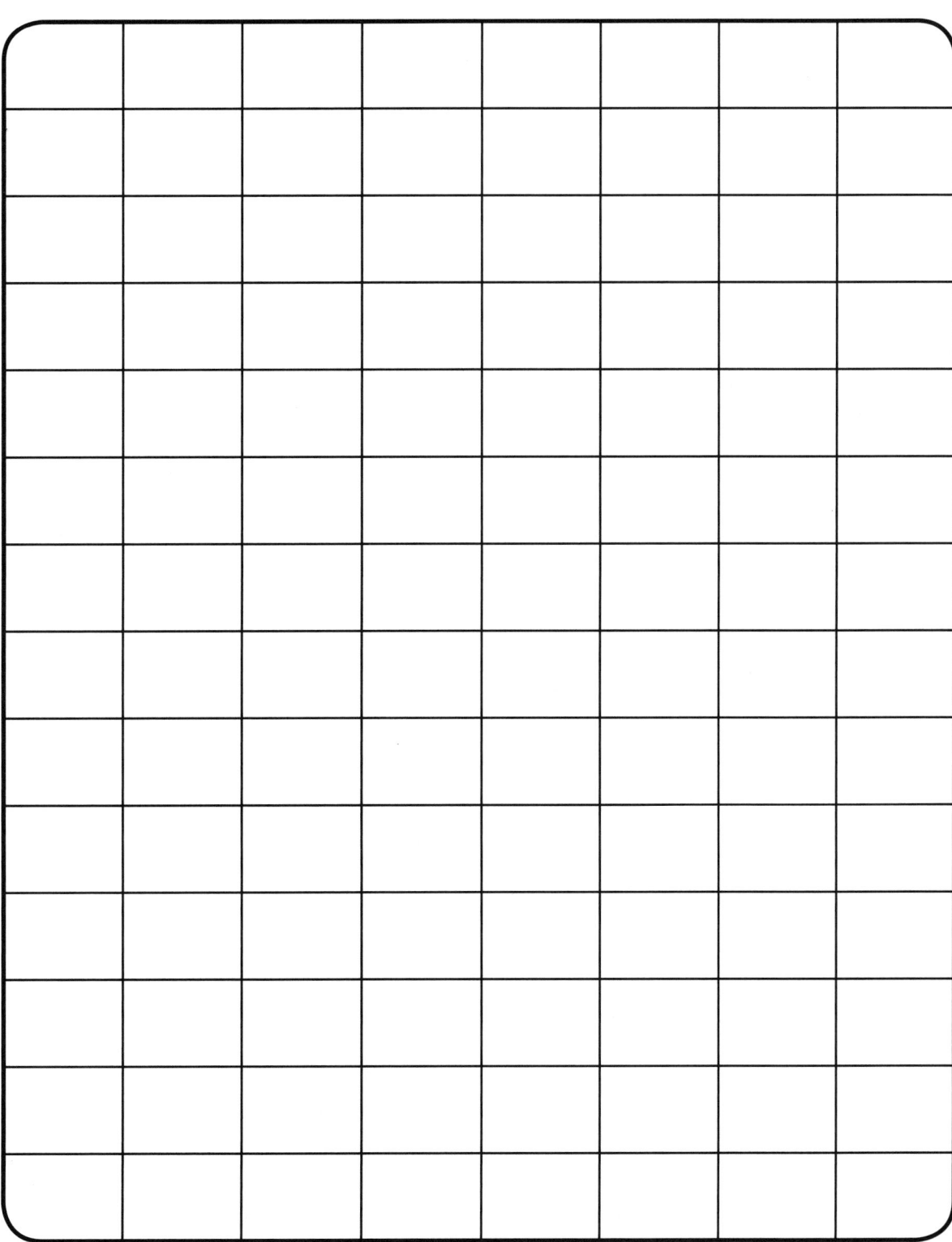

Four in a Row

With a partner, take turns writing an X or O in each circle. The person who gets four in a row first wins.

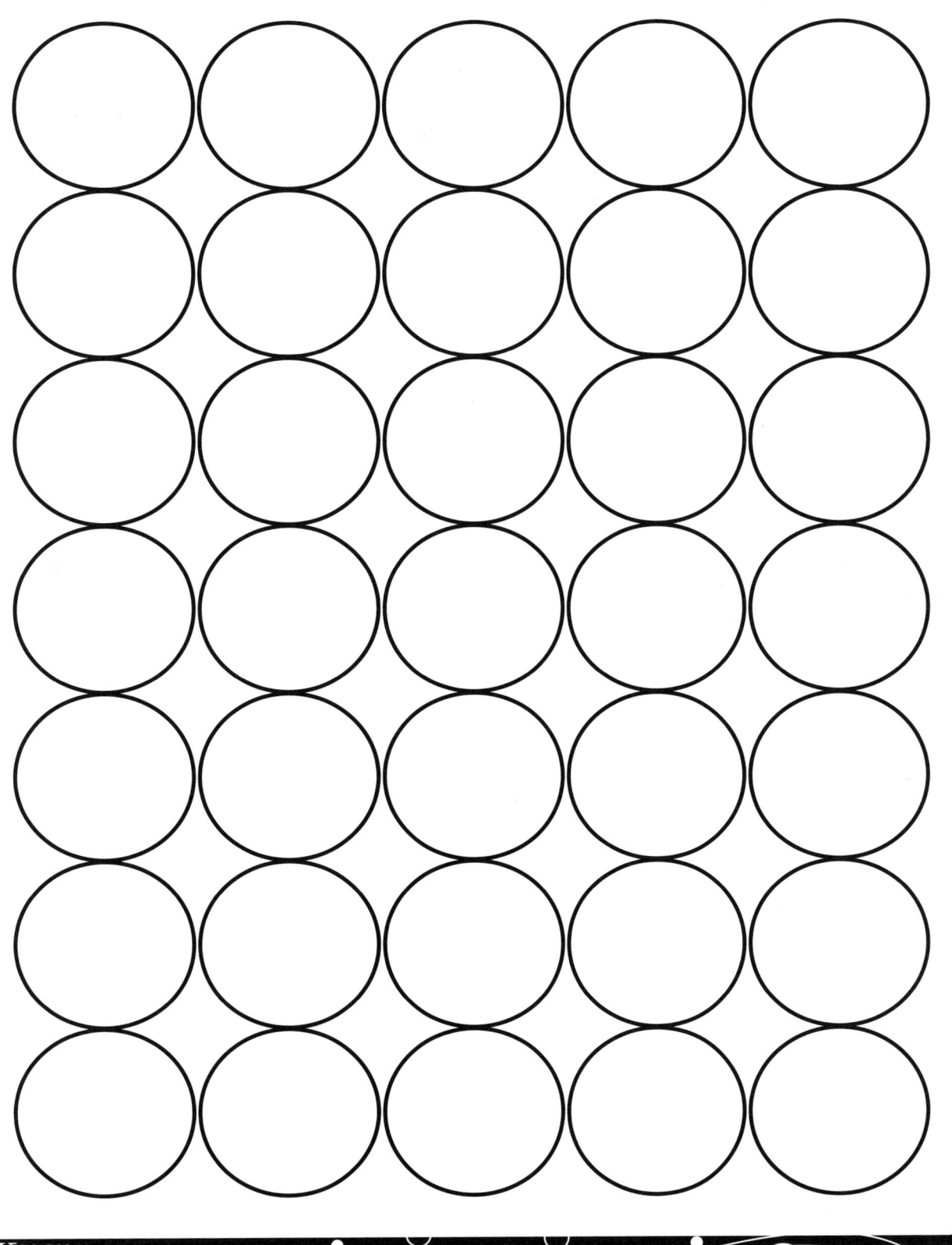

Hangman

Select a secret word. In the Word box, draw one horizontal line for each letter of the word. Have your opponent try to guess the word by guessing letters. At the bottom, cross off the letters your opponent guesses. Write the letters your opponent guesses correctly on the lines in the Word box. For each incorrect guess, draw one part of the hangman. See if your opponent can guess the word before you complete the hangman stick figure.

Word

A B C D E F G H I J K L M

N O P Q R S T U V W X Y Z

Making Words

Fill in the grid with letters from the alphabet in random order.

Make words using linking letters from the grid.

My Words

Pipe Layer

To win, a player must connect his or her dots from one side of the board to the other. Lines may only be horizontal and vertical and may not cross your opponent's line.

Sudoku 4x4

Use this grid to play Sudoku. Fill out a complete grid so that each column, each row, and each block contains all the digits 1–4. Erase some cells or partially fill out another grid and give it to a partner to solve for the missing numbers.

Sudoku 6x6

Use this grid to play Sudoku. Fill out a complete grid so that each column, each row, and each block contains all the digits 1–6. Erase some cells or partially fill out another grid and give it to a partner to solve for the missing numbers.

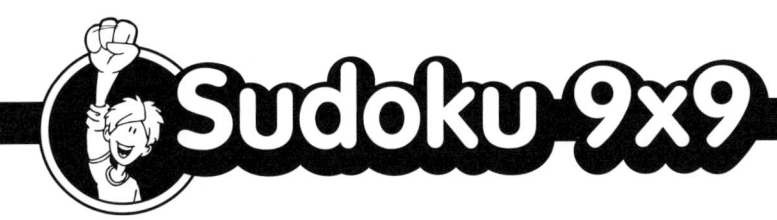

Sudoku 9x9

Use this grid to play Sudoku. Fill out a complete grid so that each column, each row, and each block contains all the digits 1–9. Erase some cells or partially fill out another grid and give it to a partner to solve for the missing numbers.

Kagan SwitchBoard

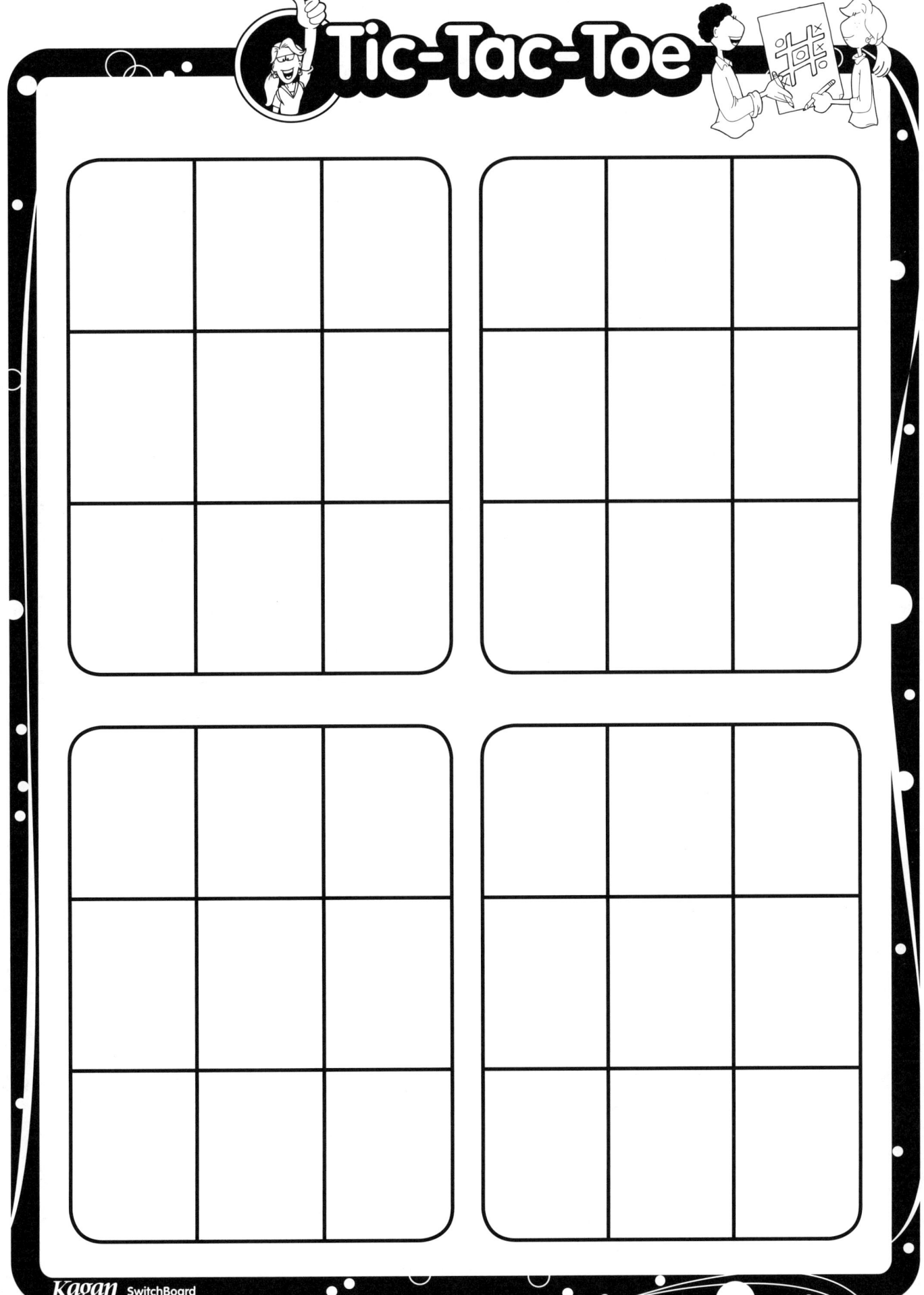

# Notes

# Notes

# Notes

Kagan
It's All About Engagement!

Kagan is the world leader in creating active engagement in the classroom. Learn how to engage your students and you will boost achievement, prevent discipline problems, and make learning more fun and meaningful. Come join Kagan for a workshop or call Kagan to **set up a workshop for your school or district**. Experience the power of a Kagan workshop. **Experience the engagement!**

SPECIALIZING IN:

- ★ Cooperative Learning
- ★ Win-Win Discipline
- ★ Brain-Friendly Teaching
- ★ Multiple Intelligences
- ★ Thinking Skills
- ★ Kagan Coaching

KAGAN PROFESSIONAL DEVELOPMENT

www.KaganOnline.com ★ 1(800) 266-7576

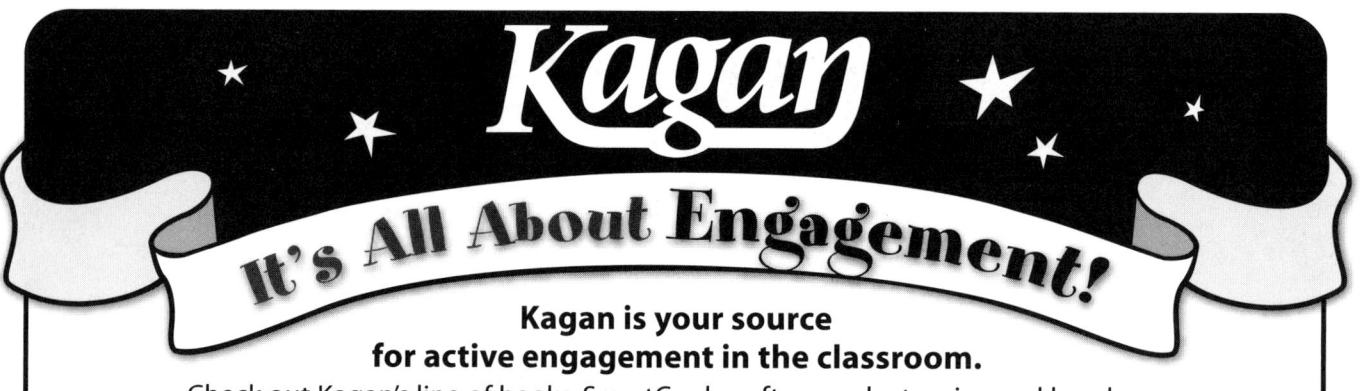

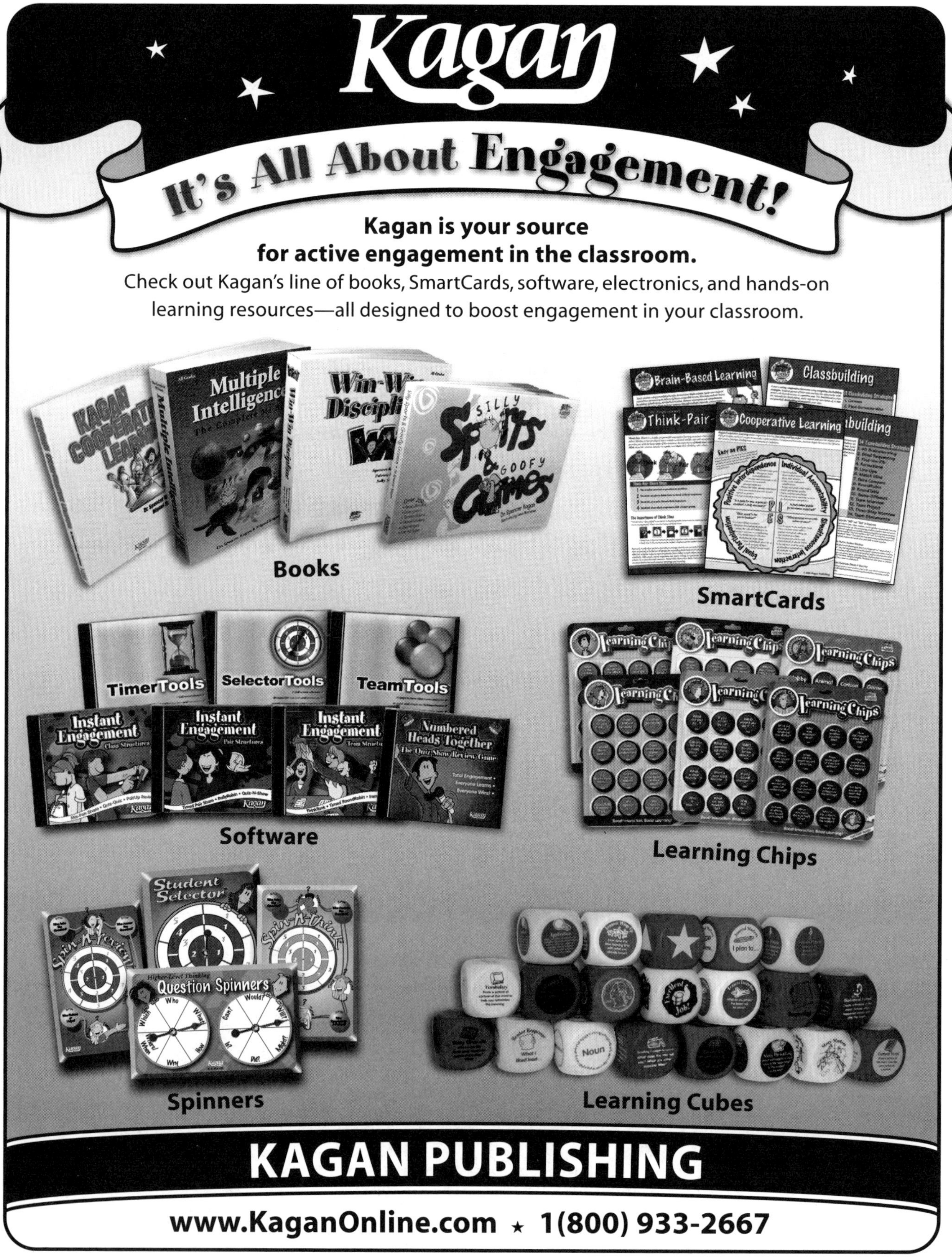
Kagan
It's All About Engagement!
Kagan is your source
for active engagement in the classroom.
Check out Kagan's line of books, SmartCards, software, electronics, and hands-on learning resources—all designed to boost engagement in your classroom.
Books
SmartCards
Software
Learning Chips
Spinners
Learning Cubes
KAGAN PUBLISHING
www.KaganOnline.com ★ 1(800) 933-2667